©2015: L. Larry Liu (self-published)
CreateSpace
Charleston, SC.
ISBN-13:978-1505429435
ISBN-10:1505429439
Hakkas in Power: A Study of Chinese Political Leadership in
East and Southeast Asia, and South America/L. Larry Liu
1. Social Science/Ethnic Studies/General (East Asia,
Southeast Asia, Latin America), 2. Political Sociology

Hakkas in Power: A Study of Chinese Political Leadership in East and Southeast Asia, and South America

By L. Larry Liu

Table of Content

Preface

The motivation for the study of Hakka political leaders derives from my interest in discovering that many of the political leaders in East and Southeast Asia were of Hakka descent. There would have been no esoteric reason for wanting to devote a whole summer to study this issue except that my family is of Hakka descent too. That was the dialect that was spoken in my house, and the distinction would have mattered little if my parents and other relatives did not draw the distinction between their own group and those of Cantonese or Mandarin speakers. In addition, as I met many other Chinese people, I realized that Hakka was a rather rare language group, and finding Hakka speakers at random outside the immediate friendship and family network would be difficult for me.

Even more important, though political talk was random and far in between in my own family, I have been absorbed with political economy problems since I was a young teenager, hanging out in my local library to absorb current political discourses in books and magazines, reading newspapers, watching political talk shows and news, and then debating and discussing that content with my teachers, friends and colleagues, and anybody that had the time and the willingness to do so. Is my political interest the reflection of my Hakka background, or am I at random one of the many other people that like to discuss politics? Such a research question would be virtually impossible to answer. But at least posing this question allowed me to get hooked to studying Hong Xiuquan's revolutionary attempt to overthrow the Qing dynasty, among other leaders.

I should perhaps also disclose the fact that there is no one that I know in my family, who has become a politician. As Hakka migrants to Calcutta (Kolkata) in India, active politics was far from the mind of my forbears. India was reeling from deep ethnic and religious-cultural tensions after independence in 1947, when Islamic-oriented Pakistan broke apart from Hindu-based India. Though there was a quite sizable Chinese population at one time in India, none of them really made it to any position of power. That was neither politically feasible, nor did they express any interest in it. They decided to focus on making money and the shoe and leather tannery businesses were important market niches which provided many Chinese in Calcutta with a solid foothold.

The 1962 border conflict between India and China certainly and very rapidly deteriorated not only the bilateral relations between these two countries, but also the political situation for many Chinese, including Hakka, in India. Some of my family's neighbors were imprisoned by the government, their property was confiscated, and they were sent to the internment camps in Rajasthan province and were held there until 1967. Travel restrictions were in place until the late-1990s, though many Chinese were capable of leaving the country for the West, especially Canada, where better economic opportunities and political freedoms were available. Only recently, with the rise and liberalization of China and to some extent India, has there been an improvement in bilateral relations and with that the treatment of the few remaining Chinese in India has improved (read the detailed ethnographic study of Hakkas in Calcutta in Oxfeld 1993; the treatment of Chinese in the prison camps can be read in Mazumdar 2010; Griffiths 2013; for the history of the border conflict read Fischer, Rose and Huttenback 1963). Given this troublesome history one could only wonder whether a Hakka in power would have made a difference in the anti-Chinese policies of the Indian government.

I do not consider myself to be the most ideal spokesperson for talking about Hakka issues, and that has to do with my lack of Chinese reading skills (which necessarily precludes me from the primary Hakka scholarship in China, despite the advances of translation services online), my lack of personal Hakka friends and other networks, my half-hearted ability to speak the Hakka language, and my personal background (I have spent my life exclusively in Europe and North America).

But personal shortcomings in ability have never inhibited the ambitions of a curious scholar, and even if the depth of scholarship that I provide in this study are minimal and shallow, I hope the reader will grow to appreciate the interesting insights they can gain from my socio-cultural study of Hakka leaders.

Hakkas in Power: A Study of Chinese Political Leadership in East and Southeast Asia, and South America

Abstract:

The Hakka Chinese have been known to have attained important political offices in East and Southeast Asia and in South America. This book contributes to the discussion of Hakka political leaders by analyzing the conditions of Hakka people in China, Taiwan, Singapore, Thailand, the Philippines and Guyana, and the rise of a few of these Hakka individuals to top leadership positions in their respective country. The argument is that despite being a minority and initially political outsiders, some of their descendants have capitalized on their outsider position to climb to the top political leadership positions.

Introduction

A common stereotype about the Hakka people is that they are fluent in many languages, or in any case have no difficulty in becoming proficient in a language different from their own. It is not surprising why that idea would be so powerful. The Hakka people are a minority anywhere they are, whether in the hill lands of Guangdong, in the outskirts of Taipei, or in the Chinatowns of Europe and the US. Therefore, they have to adjust to the majority culture, and develop an intimate knowledge of their surrounding, which includes adopting many cultural features and the local language. The assimilation to the local environment sometimes goes so far that many younger Hakkas are no longer fluent in their own dialect.

The Hakka people (客家人, Kejiaren) are one of the major ethnic groups in China, and they account for anywhere between 60 and 100 million people in the world, 90% of which are based in China (Zeng 2004). One of the distinguishing features of the Hakka people is that they are disproportionately strong represented in the ranks of political leadership both in and outside of China. Within China alone Hakka political leaders have been the backbone of many uprisings and revolutions, such as the Taiping rebellion (1850-64) and the Communist ascendance to power in 1949 (Christiansen 1998, 1; Erbaugh 1992; Wang 1992, 1994; Zhang 1994). In very simple terms, one may consider Hakkas to be the big political troublemakers wherever they currently reside in.

Most previous studies have focused on Hakka politicians and military leaders within China (especially Erbaugh 1992; Leong 1997) or Taiwan (Christiansen 1998), since that is where most of the Hakkas are located in. And some studies have looked at Hakka people worldwide, but in rather general terms rather than in terms of their political contribution (Chan 2010). There have been a few limited accounts of several Hakka leaders in several Asian countries, but with a strong focus within China (Lee 2005). But there has never been a complete account of Hakka leaders in various other countries around East and Southeast Asia and South America. This study seeks to fill the gap in the literature.

There are many examples of famous political leaders, including the leader of the Taiping rebellion, Hong Xiuquan; former president of China, Sun Yat-sen[1]; former Chinese Communist party chairman, Deng Xiaoping. Outside of China, the Hakkas also had many leaders, including former prime minister of Singapore, Lee Kuan Yew and his son and current prime minister Lee Hsien Loong; former president of Taiwan, Lee Teng-hui; current president of Taiwan, Ma Ying-Jeou; former prime minister of Thailand, Thaksin Shinawatra, and his younger sister and former prime minister, Yingluck Shinawatra; former president of the Philippines, Corazon Aquino (Christiansen 1998, 1), and former president of Guyana, Arthur Chung.[2] There is even a Hakka Supreme Court chief justice, Y.K.J. Yeung Sik Yuen, in the island of Mauritius.[3] This book will describe the conditions of the Hakkas in their respective countries (in China and the diaspora), and lay out the rise of the different Hakka political leaders in China, Taiwan, Singapore, Thailand, the Philippines and Guyana.

The study addresses three research questions:

1. Under what socio-historical circumstances did the

---

1   Though there are disputes about Sun's heritage. Luo Xianglin (1933, 263-5) asserted that he was Hakka, but Tan Bi'an (1963) disputes this.
2   A list of Hakka political leaders comes also from Wikipedia. "Hakka People." http://en.wikipedia.org/wiki/Hakka_people#Revolutionaries_and_politicians
3   "Nomination de M. Bernard Sik Yuen, en qualite de juge en chef de la Cour supreme de l'elle Maurice." Cours Judiciares Supremes Francophones. http://www.ahjucaf.org/+Nomination-de-M-Bernard-Sik-Yuen+.html For a study of the Hakkas in Mauritius and a global survey of Hakkas, read Chan (2010)

      Hakkas attain political power?
2. Who are the Hakka leaders (biographical)?
3. What kind of policies did these Hakka leaders put into place (politics, economics)?

My argument is that the Hakka political leaders were initially political outsiders, but gradually fought their way into power. The Hakkas have struggled particularly hard to succeed economically and politically where they lived, and some of their descendants have been successful in occupying the most important political offices in their respective country. Before I can turn to a detailed examination of the Hakkas in the various countries, I will first start with some historical context and describe the Hakka origins.

1: The Origins of Hakka People[4]

Hakka is one of the seven major dialects in China. The Hakka people have been widely dispersed in the southern part of China. They originally come from the Central Plain (Zhongyuan 中原) around Luoyang (洛阳) in Henan (河南), but have migrated in several waves toward the south between the third and eighth century AD. The destination provinces were mainly Guangdong(广东), Guangxi (广西) and Hainan (海南) (The area was formerly known as Lingnan province). Large migration waves also went to Taiwan and Sichuan. The densest Hakka population in the 1930s was in about two dozen counties in the border regions between Jiangxi (江西), Guangdong and Fujian (福建). Mei county (梅县) in Guangdong is considered the core settlement area of the Hakkas (Christiansen 1998, 2-3).

Genealogical research finds that Hakka genes are tilted more toward northern Han people than other southern Han people, though all Han Chinese are closely genetically related (Chen et al. 2009).[5] When the Qing dynasty brutally crushed rebellions in Fujian and Guangdong, many Cantonese had died, which opened up space for Hakkas to move in during the late 1600s (Erbaugh 1992, 948). After

---

4   A longer description of Hakka origins is available by Xie Tingyu (1929)

5   Chen et al. (2009, 783) write, "Hakka and Teochew were found to be closer to the central provinces in terms of ancestry, whereas Cantonese, being native dwellers of Guangdong, showed a degree of genetic differentiation from the other two groups. This is consistent with historical migration records that show that, from the late ninth century onward the Teochew originated from the neighboring province of Fujian, and began migrating particularly during the Song dynasty. The Hakka, who had their origins in the northern provinces, migrated to Guangdong during that time, as well as in the late 17th century, particularly during the Qing dynasty. The lack of evidence for the more northerly origins of the Hakka in our study could be attributed to the early migrations of the Hakka, such that subsequent genetic exchange between the Hakka and the local population through marriage occurred long enough to make the Hakka more similar to the southern populations (instead of to their northern ancestral populations)."

the disastrous Hakka-Punti War in the mid-1800s, the Hakkas settled in Sichuan, Hong Kong and overseas (ibid., 947). Due to their migration history, the Hakkas are referred to as the 'guest people' (the Chinese root word, kejia ren 客家人, refers to guest people). The origin of the 'Hakka' term was self-selected by the Hakkas, and came during the late-Ming dynasty, when the rulers required residents to report their ethnicity in population registers (baojia, 保甲) (Leong 1997, 65-6). Hakka people also refer to themselves as Tang 唐, rather than Han 汉 (Roberts 2003, 101).

Culturally speaking, the Hakkas not only spoke their own dialect, but they also observed their own traditional customs. They took up many of the vocations that were despised by the Puntis (the Puntis refer to the native Cantonese people), including barbers, tenant peasants, itinerant blacksmiths, stone-masons, and miners.[6] Because the Hakkas had to toil in poorer land than the native people, they were known for their firm, and strong spirit, bravery in fighting, independence and adventurousness. Their permanent resource conflicts with the Puntis made them develop a very stubborn, insubordinate fighting spirit. They had a strong nationalist sentiment, and resented Manchu rule over China (Teng 1971, 18-9). Hakkas tended to band together, and were known for their clannishness. The round community houses, called tulou, which were also built to facilitate self-defense, attests to this (Lee 2005, 65).

In the eyes of the Puntis, the Hakkas were considered as intruders, having alien speech, and outlandish social and cultural practices. Because Hakka women did not receive the then-common practice of footbinding, and were working along the men in the fields, or buy groceries in marketplaces, mixing freely with men, the native Cantonese, who considered the strict separation between the sexes to be crucial, found the Hakka to be corrupting to

---

6 The Hakka had to do these jobs in addition to working on their plots of land to supplement their meager income (see Bohr 2012, 10)

the society. The Hakka immigrants in turn felt ostracized by the natives, who were held together by strong kinship, territory and community ties. Pejorative ethnic labeling, the taunting of Hakka women by native men, the lack of permanent tenancy rights for Hakka people, and competition for water and other resources, had kept ethnic tensions high. But as long as the economy flourished over the centuries, the social tensions could be controlled. An economic downturn in the nineteenth century set the stage for political conflict (Leong 1997, 61-2).

A full-scale war, called the Hakka-Punti War (1855-67; 土客械斗 tuke xiedou), erupted as the economic crisis continued to wear on. The Hakkas were intensely competitive people, turning their attention toward academic success through the civil service examination system even as economic opportunities were shrinking and academic competition was increasing (Leong 1997, 61-2). Hakka-dominated Mei county had produced many successful candidates for the civil service (Christiansen 1998, 4). As immigrants, the Hakka settlements remained relatively small compared to the native Cantonese. There was strict segregation between Hakka and Cantonese settlements, and they often lived in separated villages. As late-migrants, the Hakkas were relegated to the less fertile hill lands that were owned by the Cantonese (Leong 1997, 71).

The Hakkas had to work on the less fertile land, and, in addition, pay ground rent to the Cantonese, who owned the land. Economic tensions increased over time as with a growing population, the requirement for the Hakka to gain new land increased, while Cantonese landlords continuously pressed for more ground rent from their Hakka tenants, particularly in economically challenging times (ibid., 71). Hakkas were already economically disadvantaged: in Hakka-populated western Fujian, 85% of the population were tenant farmers, who paid between 60 to 80% of their crops in rents. 90% were illiterate and 25%

were jobless wanderers (Erbaugh 1992, 949). Wherever Hakka settlement was very dense, the Hakkas organized fights and battles with the Puntis (Leong 1997, 71). The Hakkas had to fight for themselves, but the best thing they could do was to organize in God-worshiping societies that raised military units to protect the Hakka and fight the Puntis. The more affluent and land-owning Puntis were able to hire a militia and local corps to carry out the fight against the Hakka (Teng 1971, 57).

The next chapter will discuss the various political leaders in China.

2: Hakka and Politics in China

The single historical event that had propelled Hakkas to temporary political leadership was the Taiping Rebellion (1850-64; 太平天国, Taiping tianguo), which was an uprising that triggered a destructive war, primarily in Hakka-based territory in Guangxi (Leong 1997, 72). Guangxi was one of the poorest and most corrupt provinces in the empire, making it a good place to organize unrest (Teng 1971, 56). It was during a time, when the Western countries were carving up China among each other, and the ruling Qing dynasty, therefore, had to confront two enemies at the same time (Grasso, Corrin and Kort 2009, 42).

The Taiping Rebellion was eventually crushed, but some scholars argue that it laid the groundwork for modern Chinese history (Michael 1966, 3), because it was closely studied by later Communist leaders. The origin of the rebellion was in the southern provinces of Hunan and Guangxi, which were geographically and politically far removed from the Qing rulers in Beijing. The Opium War had produced significant economic dislocation. After the war many soldiers were left without any jobs, and many of them became bandits. The dislocation was aggravated by the northern movement of ports for trade. As a result, many destitute laborers and transport workers had lost their jobs too. Ethnic rivalries and foreign ideas (e.g. Christian religion among the Hakkas) exacerbated social tensions. The main rivalry was that between the Hakkas and the Puntis.

The founder of the Taiping Rebellion was a leader named Hong Xiuquan (洪秀全), who was a frustrated scholar of Hakka origin. He had failed the civil service exam four times. While studying as an academic, he had encountered Christianity. He received the vision that he was one of the younger brothers of Jesus of Nazareth, and had the mission to cleanse the world from "idolatrous demons" in order to "establish a heavenly kingdom of great peace" (太平天国 Taiping Tianguo). Hong studied the Old Testament, went to Guangxi with some followers to win over thousands of converts. Hong heavily attacked opium, gambling, drinking and other vices, and called for the equality of men and women (abolition of foot-binding and polygamy), and equal status for oppressed minorities, such as the Hakka.

Hong called for the overthrow of the Qing dynasty, which is to be replaced by a theocratic state with communal sharing of wealth, prohibiting the private accumulation of wealth. The family remained an important social unit, but all economic responsibilities were to be transferred to the state. Unfortunately, the high moral values could not be maintained, because the Taiping leaders did appropriate huge fortunes, while their followers were toiling in poverty. While the Taiping leaders prescribed chastity and sexual purity among their followers, they themselves kept harems (Hong had 88 concubines). The Taipings wanted all people to read the Bible, using a simpler vernacular writing compared to the difficult style of the Mandarinate. The separation between civil and military duties was also repealed under Taiping rule. That was a direct attack on the Confucian value system, which singled out the educated gentry elite as government officials and moral leaders.[7]

When the economic conditions continued to deteriorate, Hong and his followers organized military units to protect against the high tax burden of government officials. The military units quickly grew in ranks fueled by their religious fanaticism, and they defeated the government troops in Guangxi and Hunan in 1850. They moved beyond the Yellow River and overran Nanjing in 1853. The tide turned against the Taiping, as internal leadership dissent weakened the movement. Hong Xiuquan escaped the infighting by retreating to pursue sensual pleasures.

In addition, the Manchu rulers (Qing) decided to grant

---

7   For more details on Taiping ideology see Reilly (2004).

more power to private armies raised by Han gentry scholars to fight the Taiping. This created regional strongmen with armies that defeated the Taiping in 1864, but also weakened the Qing central government (Grasso, Corrin and Kort 2009, 42-8). Foreign powers also played a role in the defeat of the rebellion (albeit a small one). The British supplied arms and steamships for the conveyance of troops in Shanghai to oppose the Taiping. A low estimate of deaths during the Taiping rebellion run to around 20-30 million (Roberts 2003, 273-5). The Taiping rebellion sparked many other rebellions, such as the Nien, Miao, and Moslem rebellions (Teng 1971, 361-83).

The Hakkas also played an important political role during the Republican Revolution (1911-12). Of the 112 Guangdong members of the Tongmenghui[8] in Tokyo in 1905-06, 50 of them were Hakka from the Mei River valley. In the years leading up to the revolution, Hakkas were very visible in journalism, the schools and the provincial assembly. A newspaper called Zhonghua xinbao (New China Journal, 中华新报) was founded by a Hakka businessman in 1908, and its policy was to attack the old Qing regime, and act as a voice for Hakka people in the eastern part of Guangdong.

When the revolutionaries had seized political control in Guangzhou, the Hakka, Chen Jiongming, became lieutenant military governor, ruling from 1912-13 and from 1920-23. Liao Zhongkai became the minister of finance; Deng Geng became the army minister; Qiu Fengjia became the education minister; Yao Yuping became the marshal of Guangzhou troops; and Liu Yongfu became the commander in chief of the volunteer corps. Chaozhou, a city in southwest Guangdong, elected the Hakka member, Zhang Licun, to the top military post. In 1913, Yuan Shikai's

---

8   The Tongmenghui were a secret society founded by nationalist leader Sun Yat-sen in Tokyo in 1905. Its goal was to overthrow the Qing dynasty and replace it by a republic with nationalist, republican and socialist goals (cf. Lee and Lee 2011).

regime based in Beijing ended the revolutionary regime of Guangdong in 1913. But political and military power in Guangdong continued to be in the hands of the Hakkas, including Zhang Fakuo (1927-28), Chen Mingshu (1929-31), and Chen Jitang (1931-36). The combined army of the three Hakka generals, Chen Jitang, Chen Mingshu and Zhang Fakuo made up about 150,000 to 160,000 men in 1932, which were very important for the nationalists in their war with Japan. Other political leaders included provincial chairman Lin Yungai, and the head of the civil administration Lin Yizhong (Leung 1997, 85-91).

With the rise of the Nationalist (国民党, Kuomintang) government under Sun Yat-sen and Chiang Kai-shek[9] beginning in the 1920s, the relative economic and political disadvantages of the Hakka disappeared. The higher social status of the Punti was diminished through the rise of nationalism and Mandarin as the national language, which created a status above the dominant Cantonese. Mandarin was about equidistant to both Hakka and Cantonese. With these Hakka gains in place, Punti's public anti-Hakka expressions came to an end, but it did not entirely eradicate Punti resentment (Christiansen 1998, 5-6). On the other hand, strong Han nationalism has made the official discourse in the country neglect the Hakkas as an important element in Chinese political society (Erbaugh 1992, 939),

---

9   Both political leaders married one of the three Soong sisters, who were Hakkas. Their father was a well-educated Methodist Bible publisher, who sent his sons and daughters to America to become educated. The oldest sister, Soong Ailing, married the richest man in China at that time and finance minister H.H. Kung. The Kung couple moved to America after the defeat of the Kuomintang in mainland China. The second sister, Soong Qingling, married Sun Yat-sen. After Sun's death, Qingling supported the Communists and later became an influential party member. The third sister, Soong Meiling, married Chiang Kai-shek, who became president of Taiwan after his defeat in the Civil War. The Soong sisters also had a brother, Soong Tse-Ven, who was the prime minister of China in 1930 and 1945-7. Carrie Gracie, "The Soong Sisters: Women of Influence in China." BBC News, October 11, 2012. http://www.bbc.com/news/magazine-19910975

even as it was necessary to prevent blood feuds and ethnic conflicts (ibid., 943).

The Hakkas also played an important role in the Chinese Communist Party (CCP, 共产党, Gongchandang), who defeated the Nationalists during the Civil War in 1949 (国共内战, guogong neizhan). Mao Zedong took over with the heavy backing of the peasantry, and enthusiastic Hakka support. 3 of the 12 founding members of the CCP were Hakka (considering that Hakkas were about 3% of the total population). The Hakkas were three times as likely to occupy high government and party positions than other Han Chinese. 6 of the 9 Communist bases in southeast China were in Hakka counties. The Communists were also able to take advantage of the Hakka women, acting as reconnaissance agents and guerrilla fighters (Bohr 2012, 16-7).

Even during the early Republic in the 1920s, many Hakka workers became supporters of the Communists. The Hakka rickshaw pullers from Guangzhou became members of the Communist union. Anarchist unions organized Hakka barbers and tea-house clerks. In Shanghang, Fujian and Anyuan, Jiangxi, mining workers were very militant and organized strikes. They were organized with the help of the Hakka labor organizer Li Lisan. Many Hakka farmers (80% of the population were peasants) were strongly penetrated by Communist organization. Communism was a popular idea among the Hakka peasants, because it promised land revolution, i.e. a redistribution of land from the Puntis to the Hakkas (Erbaugh 1992, 954-6). Many of the Communist leaders were, in fact, Hakkas. Zhu De, Chen Yi and Ye Jianying were marshalls in the People's Liberation Army (解放军, jiefangjun), which is a rank above general (ibid., 961). Zhu De and Ye Jianying were instrumental in the campaign to confiscate and redistribute land for community farming. They mobilized peasants into women's, literacy, health, education and militia programs (Bohr 2012, 16-7).

Deng Xiaoping

The most important Hakka leader in the CCP was Deng Xiaoping, who led the country after Mao's death in 1976 onward, and controlled the party at least until 1992 (for biographies consult Franz 1988; Baum 1994, Evans 1994; Deng 1995). His political success can explain a revival of Hakka studies in the PRC (Chen 2010, 74). His background and policies are worth a longer description. Deng was born on August 22, 1904 in Guang'an, a city in the eastern part of Sichuan province. His ancestors can be traced back to Hakkas residing in Mei county in Guangdong, before they undertook the migration to Sichuan 200 years before Deng's birth (Franz 1988, 10; Evans 1994, 1). Deng's father, Deng Wenming, was a mid-level landowner, who had one wife and three concubines (his wife did not bear him any children) (Franz 1988, 7). Just like many other Hakkas, who were opposed to Qing rule, Wenming had joined several anti-Qing secret societies to advocate for the downfall of the Qing (ibid., 11).

Deng Xiaoping himself became interested in politics. After receiving his education in the Chongqing Preparatory School, he lived in France between 1920 and 1926, first on a scholarship funded by a Chinese association that wanted to promote the acquisition of industrial skills among Chinese youth, which would presumably benefit China in its own development. But barely a few months into the program, the association ran out of money and the Chinese students, including Deng had to fend for themselves (Evans 1994, 14-5). Deng and the other students dropped out of school, and had to take low-paid factory jobs. Of the 1,500 Chinese students in France only 300 had found factory jobs (Franz 1988, 26). And those that found jobs received only half of a Frenchmen's salary.

No wonder that Deng and other students turned to Marxism and Communism, which was strongly represented in French politics, especially after the Bolshevik Revolution

in Russia. Under the direction of older students, Zhao
Shiyan and Zhou Enlai, Deng studied Marxism (Evans 1994,
17). In 1924, Deng became a member of the Central
Organization of the CCP in Europe (Franz 1988, 44). In
1926, Deng moved to Moscow in Russia to study more
socialist thought in the Sun Yatsen University (Evans 1994,
29).

In 1927, Deng returned to Xian, China to become part of
the Sun Yatsen Political and Military Academy, which at
that time harbored both Communists and Nationalists. But
Chiang Kai-shek and a group of Nationalist politicians
decided to purge Communists from the ranks of the
academy. Many large landowners were also reluctant to
support an organization, whose members demanded land
confiscation and redistribution (ibid., 40-1). Deng escaped
Xian and left for Wuhan to join the Communist party
bureaucracy (ibid., 43).

Chiang Kai-shek decided to root out the Communist base
in Jiangxi in 1934. This forced the Communists to retreat to
the northern province of Shaanxi in the year-long Long
March (长征 changzheng) (ibid., 65-7). Of the 86,859 Red
Army soldiers that began the march only 9,000 survived
(Franz 1988, 96). The Nationalists might have gone on to
eliminate even the Communist base in Shaanxi, but in 1937
the Japanese invaded China, forcing the two sides to work
together. Deng became political commissar and
commandeered an army division in the area bordering
Shanxi, Henan and Hebei provinces (ibid., 107). After the
Japanese defeat in 1945, the Civil War resumed, and Deng
as propaganda master and Commissar of the Second Red
Army disseminated the ideas of Mao Zedong to help defeat
the Nationalists.

In October 1949, Deng was appointed mayor of
Chongqing. He became the vice chairman of the regional
commission and first secretary of the regional party bureau
in the south-west. The goal was to establish law and order,
to promote economic recovery and to carry out land reform

(Evans 1994, 108-9). Only three years later, in July 1952, he was transferred to Beijing to serve as deputy premier and vice president in the committee of finance (ibid., 115). As a major leader in the Communist party, next to Mao Zedong and Zhou Enlai, Deng steadfastly supported the extreme position of land collectivization with Liu Shaoqi, another party veteran, being the only major opponent, who had thought that things had to be planned more carefully. It was not until the early 1960s that Deng switched his views to Liu's side, which made Deng, in turn, unpopular in the party leadership (Franz 1988, 136).

In the 1956 party convention, Deng was elected general secretary and a member of the standing committee being responsible for both policy-making and implementation (Evans 1994, 133). He was at the center of political affairs until the beginning of the Cultural Revolution in 1966 (ibid., 139). During the Great Leap Forward (1958-61 大跃进, dayuejin), Deng sided with Mao, supporting his approach of rapid industrialization and the creation of communes (ibid., 148-9).

The Great Leap proved ultimately very costly due to famine outbreaks, which forced the leadership, including Deng, to develop a recovery program to shift from an emphasis on heavy industry to light industry and agriculture (ibid., 161-2). The apparent failure of the Great Leap made Deng very suspicious about Mao's approach of maximizing the participation of the workers in management decisions, the equalization of pay rates and greater reliance on non-material incentives (ibid., 164-5).[10] Deng had thought that in order to end the famine, grain production had to increase, and material incentives for farmers were really important to achieve that goal. In his words, "Whether the cat is white or black is irrelevant so long as the mice are caught." (Franz 1988, 157).

Mao became alienated from Liu and Deng, and turned

10 The criticism of the Great Leap Forward can be read in Li and Yang (2005); Teiwes and Sun (1999).

against them (ibid., 161). When Mao called out the Cultural Revolution (1966-76), he had ordered the Red Guard, consisting of extremist youth, to attack his political opponents and strengthen his own position. After initial appeasement, Deng spoke out against what he considered violent acts perpetrated against innocent people for which he was promptly rebuked by the pro-Mao faction (ibid., 189-90). In order to survive, Deng issued a long self-criticism, decrying his own "false, bourgeois line" (ibid., 191). But it did not help him.

The furious Red Guard attacked Deng and Liu in speeches and speaking choruses; and Mao organized a censure vote against them to remove them from the Standing Committee (ibid., 195). Deng was humiliated in his villa; bent his back, stretched arms behind him, lowered the head to his knees, and listened to inflammatory tirades by the Red Guard. Liu was mistreated even worse. He was dragged to a mob, tortured and imprisoned such that he died two years later in a prison in Kaifeng, Henan province (ibid., 198). The campaign against Liu and Deng were organized by Mao's wife, Jiang Qing, in addition to Kang Sheng, Chen Boda and Zhang Chunqiao (Evans 1994, 183).

Deng escaped Liu's fate by being taken away from his official residence into a small house, after which the campaign against him died down (ibid., 184). After two years, he was transferred into a labor camp in Jiangxi, doing physical labor as a form of punishment (ibid., 186). What brought Deng out of political obscurity was the death of his opponent Lin Biao, who had originally been Mao's favored successor, but, who soon fell out of his favor. Deng immediately requested a return to Beijing, and was granted vice premiership upon return in 1974 with the help of his friend, premier Zhou Enlai (ibid., 190). He took over the foreign affairs portfolio, and worked on improving US-China relations (ibid., 198-99).

By the end of 1975, the tide had again turned against Deng, because Mao thought that Deng wanted to undermine his Cultural Revolution, even though Deng took good care in justifying his policies with reference to statements made by Mao (ibid., 206). With the Tiananmen incident, where thousands of protesters criticized the government, the Gang of Four, led by Jiang Qing, organized a campaign for the fall of Deng, who immediately escaped to Guangdong hiding his whereabouts from the Gang of Four (ibid., 212). But Deng's situation improved after the death of Mao in September 1976. Premier Hua Guofeng pushed for the imprisonment of Jiang and the gang (ibid., 215-6). With the gang out of the way, Deng was rehabilitated in his party leadership positions on July 1977 (Franz 1988, 260). In the party plenary session on December 1978, Deng catapulted himself to become the leader of the party, ousted his rival Hua, and appointed his associates and loyalists to the important politburo positions (ibid. 267-8).

Deng Xiaoping is known for his economic reforms beginning in the late-1970s, which had propelled China from an underdeveloped socialist country into a highly developed and wealthy society, taking advantage of land de-collectivization, which allowed farmers to privately and independently till their land for profit, and thereby massively increase agricultural productivity (ibid., 286-88; Naughton 1995, 67). Deng's next goal was to further mechanization and heavy industry, and expand employment in labor-intensive light manufacturing and service jobs in urban areas (Naughton 1995, 77). Unprofitable enterprises, that were previously propped up by state subsidies, were shut down (ibid., 84). Privatization was advanced by reducing and abolishing state monopolies, relaxing restrictions on activities in the private sector and allowing the entry of private firms into the market (Yip 2006, 51; also discussed in Liu 2013).

During the early years of his reform, Deng had shown a strong interest in education, science and technology, which he thought were crucial factors in the development of China (Evans 1994, 225). In terms of political reform, Deng insisted on removing the social labeling of landlords and capitalists, and tight control of private life and hobbies, which had been so pervasive during the Cultural Revolution. He also pushed for the retirement of senior party leaders (ibid., 257). In terms of foreign policy, Deng prioritized the re-integration of Hong Kong and Macao into China, (ibid., 263) which happened in 1997 and 1999 respectively.

The economic reforms have made China a more prosperous country, yet corruption and inequality have arisen as enormous challenge (on corruption: Sun 2004; Wederman 2004; on inequality: Gustafsson, Li, Sicular 2010; Li, Sato, Sicular 2013). It was Deng himself, who had approved of some people getting rich first (quoted in Shawki 1997), but he had also made clear in an April 1987 statement that "[i]f we adopted the capitalist system in China, probably fewer than 10 per cent of the population would be enriched, while over 90 per cent would remain in a permanent state of poverty. If that happened, the overwhelming majority of the people would rise up in revolution. China's modernization can be achieved only through socialism and not capitalism." (Deng 1987, 184) This statement should be rather prescient.

Only two years later, in 1989, with more intellectual freedom available to students and intellectuals than ever before, yearning for more democratic rights, with the fall of the Eastern European communist governments sending shock waves through the world, with rising job insecurity fears among state-sector workers, with growing peasant resentment against wealthier urban residents and cash crop earners, and with the death of politburo veteran Hu Yaobang (who was popular among students), a large number of students had gathered on Tiananmen Square to attack corruption, the bureaucracy and demand democracy (Evans 1994, 288-9).

The student movement had started in April 1989, and gathered more steam and more protesters in May (ibid.,

293). General secretary Zhao Ziyang had taken a conciliatory position, and was sympathetic to the student protesters. Premier Li Peng (a Hakka) and Deng Xiaoping (who was then only the chairman of the military commission, but with the power to summon the military forces) were the hardliners, who thought that the Tiananmen protests were a direct threat to the CCP. Li and Deng prevailed, and declared martial law. Deng, believing that police was insufficient to handle the more than 300,000 protesters in Beijing (Vogel 2011, 617), traveled to the provinces to drum up military troops to march to Beijing and smash the Tiananmen protests, which occurred on June 3 and 4 resulting in more than 3,000 deaths and the exiling of numerous students and intellectuals (Evans 1994, 294-8).

Politically, the crackdown at Tiananmen meant the end of Zhao Ziyang's political career, who had been designated Deng's successor. The job of general secretary was given to Jiang Zemin (ibid., 301), who later also became the president. Only a few months after the Tiananmen protests, Deng resigned from his chairmanship of the military commission, but stayed on as influential adviser to the government (ibid., 303). He toured the country in 1992, giving speeches along the way, and warned about 'leftists' (i.e. the Tiananmen protesters), who are blocking China's road to progress. "The opinion which equates reform and opening to ushering in and developing capitalism, and which holds that the danger of peaceful evolution mainly comes from the economic field, precisely represents leftism." (ibid., 307) He died on February 19, 1997.

Recent Developments for Hakka

In the early years of Communist rule, the success of Hakka politicians has not necessarily yielded in the prosperity of rural Hakka peasants. The so-called Third Front industrial development between 1964-71 was a government policy to improve the lot of rural peasants. China, which had felt threatened militarily from abroad, had decided to move heavy industry further inland. Railway lines and factories were also moved inland, benefiting provinces like Sichuan, Fujian and Guangdong, and especially regions with heavy Hakka settlement.

But Third Front investments were terminated in the 1980s, because they were no longer viable economically. Meixian prefecture which includes the poorest counties of Guangdong remained largely poor, exporting many migrants overseas (Erbaugh 1992, 964-5).

However, the most recent development of Meizhou city, the heartland of the Hakkas, has been marked by progress. In 2003, total export and import was $300 million, and foreign investment was $168 million. The city is reliant on their key energy, transportation, hi-tech, electronic component, agro-technology, processing, real estate, mineral resource (coal, iron mine, manganese) and tourist industry.[11] The city's annual economic growth was 10.7% in 2012.[12] Public discussion of the Hakkas is becoming increasingly common, because they are no longer considered a threat. But the old Hakka leaders are beginning to die off, while the national culture is becoming more homogeneous (ibid., 966). The explicit Chinese government policy has been to promote a harmonious

---

11 Internet Archive. "Investment Environment: Meizhou City." http://web.archive.org/web/20061014114829/http://www.gddoftec.gov.cn/sq/en/tz_mz.html
12 China Knowledge. "Meizhou (Guangdong) City Information." http://www.chinaknowledge.com/CityInfo/City.aspx?Region=Coastal&City=Meizhou

society, and "depoliticize" ethnic and cultural differences (see Xie 2014).

The home base for Hakka political leaders remains Guangdong province, where a so-called "Hakka Gang" has continuously ruled the province (Minahan 2014, 89). Chen Yu was the governor of Guangdong (1957-67)[13], and so were Ye Xuanping (1983-5)[14] and Huang Huahua (2003-2011).[15]

Hakkas in Hong Kong

There has also been a sizable portion of Hakkas that live in Hong Kong. According to an 1819 gazette, there were 570 Punti and 270 Hakka settlements in the Hong Kong district (Ng 1983, 84). The first Hakkas settled in Hong Kong following the Qing dynasty's evacuation order, which was meant to weaken anti-Qing forces (Hase 1995). Farming used to be the traditional Hakka occupation, and it was mostly done by women, because the men were looking for labor jobs in the city.

By the 1970s, agriculture had declined in many Hakka villages, and more educational opportunities meant that more people could become educated and have career mobility. More Hakkas have either moved abroad or into the city (Gao 1997). Hakka culture seems to be disappearing, because apparently no child under 12 still speaks Hakka (Lau 2005). While older generations (born before 1950) of Hakkas have a relatively strong sense of group cohesiveness resulting from their village lifestyle, where they faced numerous outside threats, younger generations, living in the modern city and being equipped with more economic opportunities, have lost this sense of cohesiveness (Leung 2012, 147).

Some contemporary Hakka politicians in Hong Kong include Martin Lee, founder of the Democratic Party (1994-

---

13 Wikipedia. "Chen Yu." http://en.wikipedia.org/wiki/Chen_Yu
14 Wikipedia. "Ye Xuanping." http://en.wikipedia.org/wiki/Ye_Xuanping
15 Wikipedia. "Huang Huahua." http://en.wikipedia.org/wiki/Huang_Huahua

2002), and a leader of the pro-democracy movement. He served in the legislative council from 1985 until 2008. He worked as a barrister before his political career, and was appointed to chair the Hong Kong Bar Association from 1980-83. Between 1985-89, Lee was part of the Basic Law Drafting Committee to give Hong Kong a post-1997 constitution, when it joined with the mainland. But he was ousted from that position following the 1989 Tiananmen crackdown.[16] Being close to the West, Beijing denounced Lee as a traitor (Jensen and Weston 2006).

Lee Wing-tat has been a member of the legislative council (1991-97; 1998-2000; 2004-2012), chairman of the Democratic Party (2004-06), and a proponent of the pro-democracy movement.[17] Tam Yiu-chung has been a member of the legislative council (1985-95; 96-98; 1998-present), and a chairman of the pro-Beijing Democratic Alliance for the Betterment and Progress of Hong Kong (2007-)[18], which holds 13 of the 70 legislative seats.

---

16 Martin Lee. http://www.martinlee.org.hk/eng/about/about.html
17 Wikipedia, "Lee Wing-tat". http://en.wikipedia.org/wiki/Lee_Wing-tat
18 Wikipedia, "Tam Yiu-chung". http://en.wikipedia.org/wiki/Tam_Yiu-chung

3: Taiwan

Of the 23 million Taiwanese, roughly 70% are Hokkien (or Hoklo/Fujianese), 15% are Hakka, less than 15% are Mainlanders, who fled China for Taiwan during the 1949 Communist revolution (mainly members of the Kuomintang), and the remainder were the aborigines (原住民 yuanzhumin) (Chan 2010, 75). Hokkien and Hakka people, who became Taiwanese, had migrated mainly from Fujian and Guangdong province during the Qing dynasty, though early Hakka settlements in southeast Taiwan can be traced back to the year 1000. A large wave of Hakka settlement occurred after the unsuccessful Taiping rebellion in the 1860s (Copper 2013, 13).

The Hakkas, as guest people, were in direct conflict with the aborigines, with whom they were in close contact, and especially the Fujianese, who forced the Hakka from the good farmland into the less fertile hill areas. This situation led to frequent fights between the two groups. One of the conflicts on February 28, 1947 escalated, leading many Fujianese to kill Hakkas (ibid., 74). Many Taiwanese were attacking Mainlanders for their bad administration, which grew into a full-scale riot. Chiang Kai-shek and the Nationalists dispatched 13,000 military personnel to Taiwan to put down the uprising, but they made things worse by shooting and bayoneting men, raping women and looting homes and shops, and then imprisoning, torturing and killing the educated classes in Taiwan, such as professors, students, judges, lawyers and doctors (Tsai 2005, 63-65).

Currently, due to a high degree of intermarriage among all the groups it is not easy to distinguish between the various cultural and ethnic groups. A lot of Mainlanders, who had entered Taiwan between 1945 and 1951, were Hakkas as well, such that ethnic divisions are not clear-cut (Christiansen 1998, 17). During Japanese rule from 1895 to

1945, Japanese language and culture were transmitted to the Taiwanese, such that Japanese became the language of communication, while the mother tongue was only spoken at home. This blurred the line between the Hokkien (who spoke Minnan), Hakka, and the aborigines.

When the Kuomintang took over Taiwan, they banned Japanese, and instead implemented Mandarin as the lingua franca. The Hokkien responded by demanding their own cultural rights, while the Aborigines resisted Mainlander assimilation. The Hakkas, on the other hand, were fairly ambivalent about Mainland influence, with some considering themselves Taiwanese, some Chinese, and some identifying as both (Chan 2010, 76). Taiwanese Hakka are said to have great admiration for Sun Yat-sen, Deng Xiaoping, and Lee Kuan Yew, who are fellow Hakkas (Copper 2013, 75).

The Nationalist Mainlanders had tight control over Taiwan's politics, economy and society, which made it difficult for non-Mainlanders to join the political and economic elite (Chang 1994). But with increasing economic and social development, the growth of a Taiwanese middle class, a changing international environment, the normalization of Western relations with the People's Republic of China, PRC, the improvement in the relationship between Taiwan and PRC in the 1980s, substantial Taiwanese investments flowing into the Mainland, and Communism collapsing, Taiwan became more democratic, reducing the distance between the Taiwanese and the Mainlanders.

Homogenizing education, public culture and increased intermarriage reduced the divide between Taiwanese and Mainlanders (Christiansen 1998, 17). A survey in the late 1980s finds that 32% of Hakka respondents' children do not know Hakka (Kiang 1991, 123). Due to better business and job opportunities an estimated 3 million Taiwanese live in Mainland China (Copper 2013, 11).

Lee Teng-hui

It was president Chiang Ching-kuo's hand-picked successor, Lee Teng-hui (1988-2000), who had embarked on the path of political reforms and democratization. Lee himself was a Hakka, and was the first to become ROC president (Chen 2010, 77). Lee became the first democratically elected president in 1996 (Tyler 1996). Lee was born in 1923 to a rural family in Sanzhi, Taipei County (Tsai 2005, 21). During the Japanese occupation of Taiwan, he went to Japanese schools, and was profoundly influenced by Japanese culture (ibid., 24). He was one of only four Taiwanese students in a high school that was dominated by the Japanese.[19]

In 1943, he enrolled in Kyoto Imperial University on a scholarship, studying agricultural economics (ibid., 42), but was particularly fascinated by Marxist theorists like Kawakami Hajime (ibid., 43), though he had no problem to shift to a more Western liberal ideology and join the Kuomintang later (ibid., 58). After serving in the Japanese army toward the end of the war, he returned to his native Taiwan to continue his studies at National Taiwan University (ibid., 56), gaining a bachelor's degree in agricultural economics in 1949, and worked as a teaching assistant at NTU (ibid., 71).

After his marriage and the birth of his son, he received a US state department scholarship to study at the Iowa State College to receive a master's degree in agricultural economics (ibid., 78). Upon return, he was promoted to an instructor at NTU (ibid., 85). While Lee lived a quiet academic life, the "White Terror" unleashed by Chiang Kai-shek's regime against the Taiwanese public, made life in Taiwan very insecure (ibid., 87). Lee was appointed a technician in the Sino-American Joint Commission on Rural Reconstruction, after which Cornell University and

---

19 Your Dictionary, "Lee Teng-hui Facts." http://biography.yourdictionary.com/lee-teng-hui

the Rockefeller Foundation offered him to attend a PhD program in 1965 (ibid., 95).

Upon return to Taiwan, he was promoted to become a senior project specialist at the Division of Rural Economics beside his teaching duties (ibid., 100). He was interrogated by KMT authorities for over a week, questioning him about his association with the Communists, but only three years later he was appointed to Chiang's cabinet as an agricultural expert (ibid., 102) thanks to his stellar academic research and reputation (ibid., 106).

Lee had made some sensible economic policy suggestions to contribute to Taiwan's economic development. He argued that Taiwan's wealth can only increase with an increase in agricultural productivity, and this can only be realized by increasing the cash incomes of farmers by letting the crop prices fluctuate based on the market, and paying the farmers in cash than in-kind. Increased agricultural production would create savings, which would underwrite industrial development, and it would increase exports, earning Taiwan the necessary foreign exchange reserves to purchase industrial machinery. Finally, it would increase government revenues in the form of agriculture taxes, which could finance industrial development too (ibid., 107). Chiang Ching-kuo welcomed this needed expertise, and made him a cabinet member in 1972. To join the cabinet, Lee also joined the KMT (ibid., 109-110).

Lee was immediately charged with improving agricultural policy, and went to Japan to study how they accomplished agricultural reform. The Japanese sacrificed the well-being of the farmers, whose land was converted to industrial zones, to benefit the conglomerates, and Lee was determined to avoid that same outcome in Taiwan by arguing for a more balanced approach of agricultural and industrial growth (ibid., 114).

Lee prioritized a gradual transitioning into an urbanized, industrial society by mechanizing agriculture and training farmers to take on new employment in the countryside. In addition he prioritized the improvement of the rural infrastructure, building of schools, paved roads, running water, irrigation system and flood control (ibid., 115-6). Coupled with export industry promotion, Taiwan's economy soared, generating more than 8% annual growth from 1952 to 1986 (ibid., 120). Because Lee quickly had gained the trust of Chiang, he was appointed mayor of Taipei in 1978, prioritizing on improving public safety and promoting Taipei's cultural life (ibid., 123-4).

In 1981, Lee was promoted the governor of Taiwan, the largest province of the island (ibid., 126). Lee's record as governor was mixed. As agriculture became mechanized, and the diversity of food stuff increased, people consumed relatively less rice, which led to a decline in food prices. In addition, the size of farms continued to shrink as parents divided the property among their children. Rather than creating well-off farmers, as Lee intended, many farmers became dependent on their children, who supplied them with income earned from city jobs (ibid., 141).

Manufacturing workers were low paid and the working conditions were substandard, which was deliberate KMT policy to attract foreign capital and was anxiously enforced via martial law, which prohibited labor unions (ibid., 142). On the other hand, there was an increase in the number of professional workers, even though their quality standards were relatively low. Lee also had close relations with big businesses and elites, despite his public sympathy for workers and peasants (ibid., 143).

Lee took credit during his tenure as governor for enforcing the clean-up of the heavily polluted Tamsui river (ibid., 144). In 1984, Lee was appointed vice president, becoming the second most powerful person in the country after Chiang Ching-kuo (ibid., 149). By that time, Chiang was already very sick, and delegated more tasks to Lee and other high-ranking officials (ibid., 150). Chiang died in January 13, 1988 of diabetes, and so Lee was sworn in as president of ROC (ibid., 159-60).

On top of Lee's agenda as president was the consolidation of his power in the KMT, the successful transition into democracy, handle relations with mainland China, break Taiwan's diplomatic isolation, and reduce the nation's over-reliance on the US (ibid., 165). After consolidating his power base, he was able to appoint younger Taiwanese to top political posts, which had been dominated by Mainlanders (ibid., 168).

After the repeal of martial law in 1987 and Lee's ascendancy to the presidency, many Taiwanese staged wave after wave of protests with issues as far-ranging as promoting the rights of aborigines, farmers, fishers and labor organizations to electoral reform (ibid., 169-70). Lee also promoted close economic relations with the former Soviet bloc countries, and increased investments into Southeast Asia (ibid., 174-5), Africa and the Middle East (ibid., 195). Lee also pushed for closer economic cooperation with Mainland China, which became Taiwan's largest trading partner in 2002 (ibid., 180).

His government lifted restrictions on investment into the Mainland, and cross-strait marriages, reduced wire-tapping and surveillance activities on the Taiwanese population, eased restrictions on demonstrations and public assemblies, and pardoned former dissidents against the KMT regime (ibid., 182-3). But Mainland relations soured temporarily with Lee's unannounced visit to Cornell University, his alma mater, where he gave a speech (ibid., 197). Lee's administration allowed the first Yuan (parliamentary) elections to be held in 1992 (ibid., 184), and the first presidential election in 1996, which he promptly won (ibid., 200).

After a major 1999 earthquake, which many Taiwanese believed to be incompetently handled by the KMT government, DPP's Chen Shui-bian won the 2000 presidential elections, with the KMT candidate Lien Chan, winning a mere 23% of the national vote (ibid., 212). After Lee's retirement in 2000, he retreated from public life, but continued to receive guests, write speeches and manuscripts, and engage in other public activities (ibid., 213).

Taiwanese Hakka Politicians

Under Lee Teng-hui's government, a multicultural Taiwan was defined as a new identity as opposed to Mainland culture only. It implemented a Hakka promotion policy, whereby Hakka is taught in elementary schools. In Hakka villages the dialect is taught as a mother tongue. The government has also invested in the training of teachers, publication of Hakka text books and research in the Hakka dialect (Chen 2010, 77). A Hakka museum was opened in Meinung township, Gao Xiong county to preserve Hakka culture and serve as a community center for local Hakka residents. Presidential candidates like James Soong have used the Hakka dialect to appeal to Hakka constituents, and they have played a crucial role in securing the election of the Democratic Party in 2000 and 2004, the first opposition party to the Kuomintang to rule the presidency (ibid., 78). Nonetheless, the Democratic Party mainly consists of Fujianese (Copper 2013, 75).

Hakkas themselves have joined politics in large numbers. To name a few examples: Wu Po-hsiung was the former interior minister (1984-88), mayor of Taipei (1988-90), Secretary General to the President (1991-96) and Chairman of the KMT (Kuomintang) (2007-09).[20] Lien Chan, was the premier of ROC (1993-97), Vice President (1996-2000) and Chairman of KMT (2000-05).[21] Tsai Ing-wen was the vice premier under Chen Shui-bian (2006-07), the 2012 presidential candidate, and is the current chairwoman of the opposition Democratic Progressive Party (2008-12, 2014-).[22] Lee Ying-yuan was a former minister of labor

---

20 Wikipedia, "Wu Po-hsiung." http://en.wikipedia.org/wiki/Wu_Po-hsiung
21 Wikipedia, "Lien Chan." http://en.wikipedia.org/wiki/Lien_Chan
22 Wikipedia, "Tsai Ing-wen". http://en.wikipedia.org/wiki/Tsai_Ing-wen

(2005-07).[23] Hsu Hsin-liang was the former chairman of the DPP (1992-93, 1996-98).[24] Huang Yu-cheng is the current minister of the Hakka Affairs Council (2008-).[25]

Ma Ying-jeou, a native Hakka born in Hong Kong, has been Taiwan's president since 2008, leading the Kuomintang. He descended from Han Dynasty general Ma Yuan and Three Kingdom era general Ma Chao in Hunan province.[26] Ma received a law degree (LLB) from National Taiwan University in 1972, and two law degrees in the US, including New York University Law School (1976, LLM) and Harvard Law School (1981, SJD). He worked as a legal consultant and associate in a Wall Street firm before returning to Taiwan as president Chiang Ching-kuo's English interpreter. He became the chair of the Research, Development and Evaluation Commission of the Executive Yuan in 1988. Three years later, he was appointed vice chairman of the Mainland Affairs Council, and began serving in the national assembly.

In 1993, Lee Teng-hui appointed him Minister of Justice, where he focused on fighting corruption, drugs, vote-buying and organized crime. He resigned office in 1997 to teach law at National Chengchi University, but returned to politics one year later as the mayor of Taipei (1998-2006). In 2005, he took over KMT chairmanship, winning 73% of the party vote. In 2007, Ma was indicted for corruption charges during his tenure as mayor of Taipei, and he resigned as KMT chairman. He was cleared from all charges in 2008, which is the same year that he won the presidency to serve as the 12th and 13th term president of ROC.

In 2008, he received 58.5% of the vote, and in 2012 51.6%. As president, Ma tried to continue to improve cross-

23 Wikipedia, "Lee Ying-yuan". http://en.wikipedia.org/wiki/Lee_Ying-yuan
24 Wikipedia, "Hsu Hsin-liang". http://en.wikipedia.org/wiki/Hsu_Hsin-liang
25 Wikipedia, "Huang Yu-cheng". http://en.wikipedia.org/wiki/Huang_Yu-cheng
26 [客家電視]專訪馬英九談客家政策(一), Youtube. December 14, 2007. http://www.youtube.com/watch?v=YxOOEf8Ck64

strait relations, but maintain the "no unification, no independence and no use of force" position of the previous administrations.[27] In 2010, the Ma administration negotiated the Economic Cooperation Framework Agreement (ECFA), which reduced tariffs on cross-strait trade (Copper 2013, 208). Ma's major challenge in the first two years of his administration was the global economic crisis, which led the economy to contract by 2% in 2009. The government responded by passing a $5.6 billion stimulus package in the form of business tax cuts, building infrastructure, and low-cost housing (ibid., 180).

The policy challenges for the government are great, because of relatively low rates of growth (Copper 2013, 179), and low wages for young workers, which spur out-migration (Lin and Teng 2014). There has been a huge growth in low wage jobs, rising to 740,000 in 2013 at average wages of NT$19,038 (US$ 641), which also has the effect of reducing salary levels for other workers. The overall average level of wages in Taiwan are lower than in Hong Kong, Singapore and South Korea. [28]

There has been a virtual stagnation of wages since the 1990s. In 1998, average monthly wages were NT$44,798, and an inflation-adjusted NT$44,739 in 2013. Worker protests in Taipei are taking action against low wages, for better labor conditions and protections, trade liberalization, privatization of state enterprises and bank mergers. Dispatch, or contract, workers are currently not entitled for benefits, bonuses, annual leave, opportunities for promotion, and can not save up to buy a house (Chen 2014). At the same time, there is a significant level of wealth inequality. With 329,000 US dollar millionaires, Taiwan boasts the eighth most number of millionaires in the

---

27 Office of the President, Republic of China (Taiwan). http://english.president.gov.tw/Default.aspx?tabid=454

28 Dawn.com. "Long Hours and Low Pay to Become the Norm in Taiwanese Labor Market." September 23, 2013. http://www.dawn.com/news/1044866

world.[29] The richest Taiwanese ($6.5 billion in 2012), Tsai Wan-tsai, who owns a banking conglomerate, is a Hakka.[30]

---

29 Taiwan Today. "Taiwan Sees Jump in Number of Millionaires." June 12, 2014. http://taiwantoday.tw/ct.asp?xitem=218527&CtNode=415

30 Taipei Times. "Fubon's Tsai family Now Taiwan's Richest: Forbes." March 9, 2012.
http://www.taipeitimes.com/News/biz/archives/2012/03/09/2003527305

4: Singapore

When Stamford Raffles, the British Lietuenant-Governor of Benkulen, landed in Singapore in 1819, making it a British colony, he found about 1,000 people living there, mostly Malays and a handful of Chinese.[31] During the early days of Chinese migration, Singapore was particularly attractive to traders, farmers and miners from Nanyang. Tan Che Sang, who had left his native Guangdong, made a fortune in Riau, Penang and Melaka, and settled in Singapore in 1819 to build the first warehouse there. Another successful and wealthy Chinese was the Hokkien Choa Chong Long, who was born in Dutch Melaka, to become the first opium revenue farmer in Singapore (Turnbull 2009, 33).

As a result of British policies to lure migration, the Singapore population increased from 16,000 in 1827 to 81,000 in 1860. By 1830, the Chinese, mostly from Fujian and Guangdong provinces, became the largest community, and by the end of Indian rule in 1867 they made up 65% of the total population in Singapore (ibid., 55). This proportion grew to three-quarters in 1914 (ibid., 114). Since most of the Chinese immigrants were laborers, women were in short supply, such that even in the mid-1860s, there were 15 Chinese men for every woman in Singapore.[32]

The Malays were humble boatmen, fishermen, woodcutter or carpenters. The Indians, mostly from the south, made up about 10% of the population, coming in as laborers, garrison troops and convicts. A small European elite, mostly British men, ruled the country as administrators and businessmen. To quote Turnbull (2009), "By the end of Indian rule, Singapore was a predominantly Chinese town, with sizable Malay and Indian

---

31 "The Malays", National Heritage Board, January 2010.
http://www.yesterday.sg/YSGPortal/
32 U.S. Library of Congress. "Singapore- A Flourishing Free Ports." 1989
http://countrystudies.us/singapore/5.htm

minorities and an upper crust composed of Europeans with a handful of wealthy Chinese, Arabs, Parsis, Indians, Armenians and Jews" (p.56).

Singapore was a very attractive trading center, trading with China, Siam, Cochin-China, and Indonesia. Chinese traders dominated Singapore's commerce, selling opium and supplies to colonies of Chinese miners and traders in exchange for gold, tin and rattan (ibid., 57). By 1880, more than 1.5 million tons of goods were passing Singapore every year (Landow 2005).

There were differences in the economic base of the various cultural Chinese groups. In Singapore and Malaysia, the Hokkien diaspora were concentrated in banking, finance, insurance, shipping manufacturing and trading, realty, building and constructions. The Teochews specialized in agricultural activities, including the planting of gambier and pepper. They also traded marine products, textiles, rice, chinaware, glassware, vegetables fish, poultry, fruits, jewelry and antiques. The Hokkien and Teochews specialized in foreign trade. The Cantonese had manually skilled occupations, including the manufacturing of furniture, leather, soy sauce, clock and watch repairs, tailoring, goldsmithery, jewelry, laundry, motor repair, engineering, drug stores and restaurants. The focus is primarily on the domestic market. The Hakkas were also very focused in crafts, including pawnbroking, retailing of Chinese herbs and medicine, textiles, shoes, jewelry, iron foundry, blacksmithery, tailoring and manufacturing of garments. The Hakkas resided in mostly rural areas and workers as manual laborers in tin mines and plantations (Hoe 2013, 44-5)

The largest ethnic groups in Singapore are the Hokkiens (30%), which is why they dominate commercial life there. The other groups include the Teochews (17%), Cantonese (15%), Hainanese (5.2%) and the Hakkas (4.6%) (ibid., 46). Among all the groups, the Hakkas were generally small and poor. The different Chinese groups had founded the

Chinese Advisory Board to air grievances to the colonial government, and they apportioned the seats based on the size of the five dialect groups.

The different groups also founded their own association to deal with cemeteries, hospitals, schools, religious festivals and social welfare issues, and include the Hokkien Association, the Cantonese Kwong Siew Association, the Hakka Huichew Association, and the Hainanese Kheng Chiu Association. New Chinese immigrants were usually socialized into their own dialect group, and they practiced de-facto segregation in work, housing, religious worship and entertainment (Turnbull 2009, 114-5). The overseas Chinese were also fairly involved in Chinese politics. The revolutionary Tongmenghui, created by Sun Yat-sen to overthrow the Qing dynasty, had founded a branch in Singapore, which became its headquarter for Southeast Asia.[33]

The Singaporean national language policy has been to promote bilingualism, whereby the three ethnic groups would learn their own language in school, in addition to English, which was the national language. The Chinese would learn Mandarin and English; the Malays English and Malay; and the Indians English and Tamil. Bilingualism has been a policy, which was introduced in order to avoid ethnic conflicts and tensions. When members of the Chinese Chamber of Commerce had asked the government to implement Chinese as the national and official language, it rejected the pleas, because it feared the country would fall apart (Chan 2010, 114-5).

Hakka is not really taught in Singaporean schools, and the identity of Hakka people is subsumed under the English and Mandarin languages (ibid., 121). Mandarin was promoted in order to break down the dialect barriers among the different Chinese groups, and it was also useful having Singaporeans communicate easily with businessmen from

---

33 US Libary of Congress. "Singapore: Crown Colony." 1989.
   http://countrystudies.us/singapore/6.htm

China, which began to develop rapidly since the late-1970s (Turnbull 2009, 315).

Lee Kuan Yew

It was in this Chinese-dominated city-state environment that Lee Kuan Yew made his rise to political leadership, serving as long-time prime minister of Singapore (1959-90), senior minister (1990-2004), and minister mentor (2004-2011). Lee is a fourth generation Hakka in Singapore. His paternal great grandfather was Lee Bok Boon, a Hakka born in 1846 in the village of Tangxi in Dabu prefecture, Guangdong. As a young man, he migrated to Singapore, where he married Seow Huan Neo, a Singapore-born Hakka girl in 1870. Only a year later, Lee's grandfather, Lee Hoon Leong, was born. In 1882, after having earned enough money, Bok Boon decided to return to China, but without his Singaporean family (Lee 1998, 26).

Hoon Leong was educated at Raffles Institution and worked as a purser on a steamer. He married Ko Liem Nio in 1899, who gave birth to a son Lee Chin Koon, or Lee's father, in 1903. Hoon Leong became prosperous after receiving an appointment as an attorney of Oei Tiong Ham, a Chinese millionaire, who made his fortune with the sugar trade in Java. The family fortune declined with the Great Depression, because rubber prices on which the family was heavily invested in declined very sharply. (ibid., 27). Chin Koon, who married Chua Jim Neo in 1922, decided to relocate his family to his father-in-law's, Chua Kim Teng, house. Chua, a Hokkien, was a rubber and property investor, and survived the depression better than Lee Hoon Leong. Jim Neo, Lee's mother, was the daughter of Chua's third wife, Neo Ah Soon, a Hakka woman. Lee Kuan Yew, born on September 16, 1923, was the oldest of five children, having three younger brothers and one younger sister (ibid., 28-9).

Lee was a good student, and won a scholarship to Raffles

Institution, the premier English-language secondary school, which only took the best students (ibid., 36). After narrowly escaping an assassination campaign by the Japanese during their occupation of Singapore (ibid., 56), Lee got a job as a clerk in the Japanese military department, and later in the Hodobu office, the English-language Japanese propaganda department (ibid., 62-3). By mid-1944, his salary was no longer sufficient due to high inflation. He sold gums on the black market to survive (ibid., 66).

Soon after the war, Lee set sail to study law first in LSE then in Cambridge, England (ibid., 99, 104). He listened to Marxist lectures, and became skeptical about British colonialism (ibid., 113). Lee gathered his first political experience in Britain, supporting the Labour Party (ibid., 124). After his bar exam in 1950, he returned back to Singapore (ibid., 126), where he promptly got a job at the law firm Laycock & Ong (ibid., 134). In 1951, Lee campaigned for his boss, John Laycock, member of the Progressives, but was soon upset about the slow pace of progress, thinking that it was not enough that the English political elite would only rule on its own behalf instead of benefiting the whole country (Turnbull 2009, 250).

Lee built his own political network, especially among extremist Chinese student leaders and University of Malaya graduates. In 1952, Lee represented government and telecommunications employees in a labor dispute, and won heavy union and labor support after winning a case for them (ibid., 252). Lee, English-educated politicians, and other trade unionists and radicals founded the People's Action Party (PAP) in October 1954 to contest national elections the following year with Lee as the chairman of the party (ibid., 255).

But it was the leader of the Labour Front, David Marshall, who won the 1955 legislative council elections, and he became the first chief minister of Singapore. Marshall, like Lee, can be considered an outsider. While Marshall was a Sephardic Jew, Lee was a Hakka. On the other hand, their political style was different: Marshall was an emotional idealist, while Lee was a pragmatic strategist (Frost and Balasingamchow 2009, 344, 350). Marshall had campaigned on independence from Britain, a Malayanization of the civil service, expanding citizenship rights to China-born inhabitants, multilingualism in the legislature and the abolition of emergency regulations.

The PAP only received three seats in the legislature, including Lee Kuan Yew and Lim Chin Siong (Turnbull 2009, 260). In the legislative elections of 1959, Lee's PAP, carrying the votes of the overwhelming majority of the Chinese-educated electorate (though Lee and other party members were mostly English-educated), won 43 of the 51 seats in the assembly, making him the first prime minister of Singapore, since Singapore was given independence by Britain except in defense and foreign affairs (Chew 1987, 127). The British did not withdraw all of their military forces until 1971 (Omar and Chan 2009).

One of Lee's first priorities in office was to balance the budget, which led his government with the support of finance minister, Goh Keng Swee, to cut civil service salaries, which was highly unpopular (Lee 1998, 317). The PAP government transformed the social welfare department into the community development department charged with building over one hundred community centers, which gave "people something positive to do".

In order to fight unemployment, the government organized "Works Brigades", which took unemployed people, put them into semi-military uniform, house them in barracks and teach them how to farm, build roads, lay bricks and do construction work. In order to moderate labor union radicalism (on whose support Lee came to power), Lee set up an arbitration court, which made it illegal for unions to strike while arbitration proceedings were ongoing (otherwise threatening de-registration to the union), and mandated secret ballots before a strike vote rather than a show of hands after a rabble-rousing speech (ibid., 324-5).

In order to fight what the government considered to be a social vice, it prohibited pornography, striptease shows, pin-table saloons, and decadent songs (ibid., 326).

In terms of education policy, the government doubled the intake of students by splitting the existing schools into a morning and an afternoon session. Furthermore, it promoted the teaching of Malay and Chinese languages (ibid., 327). The government also launched clean-up campaigns of streets, beaches and parks, and in order to discipline civil servants and ministers, and gain public approval of the PAP government, high-ranking officials, including Lee, also participated in these campaigns (Frost and Balasingamchow 2009, 385). The government implemented a housing policy, creating the Housing Development Board, which built over 53,000 housing units between 1960 and 1965.

With respect to health policy, the government doubled health care expenditures the first five years in office, expanding the number of hospitals, maternal and child clinics, and campaigns to eradicate tuberculosis (ibid., 387). By the 1970s infant mortality and life expectancy reached western values; smallpox, cholera, diphtheria, and polio virtually disappeared thanks to the vaccination policies (Turnbull 2009, 318).

The newly created Public Utilities Board established running water, electricity, gas, better sanitation and sewage across the country (Frost and Balasingamchow., 387). To help industrialize the country, Lee granted tax exemptions to foreign investors and designated the swampland Jurong as industrial zone, promptly attracting Shell company to build an oil refinery there (ibid., 388).

In 1961, the fiercely anti-communist Malayan prime minister, Tunku Abdul Rahman, proposed the formation of a Malaysian Federation, which included Malaya, Singapore, Sabah, and Sarawak, which led the left-wing communists of the PAP coalition to leave PAP and found their own party, the Barisan Sosialis (Socialist Front), reducing Lee's comfortable majority to 26 of 51. In the next elections, in 1963, Lee's English-educated faction and the PAP secured 37 seats, which was a comfortable majority.[34]

Lee also cracked down on the Barisan party by arresting hundreds of pro-communist and anti-Malaysia activists (Chew 1987, 127-8). Barisan leader, Lim Chin Siong, was imprisoned in 1963 and not released until 1969, after which he fled to exile in London before returning to Singapore and lived a quiet life (Wong 2009). PAP consolidated its base in the state bureaucracy. Lee ensured a taming of the labor unions, and implemented education and economic policies to gain a mass political base (Chew 1987, 127-8).

Lee himself favored joining the Malaysian federation, citing economic benefits for both sides (Lee 1998, 397), and he campaigned vigorously for it by visiting all Singaporean constituencies and speaking in the native dialect of the local residents (English, Mandarin, Malay, Hokkien). On August 31, 1963, Singapore formally joined the Malaysian Federation, which was the same day that it became formally independent from Britain (Turnbull 2009, 282). But the federation lasted for a mere two years. There were bitter clashes between the pro-Malay, anti-communist Alliance, led by Tunku and the United Malay National Organization (UNMO) on the one hand, and the Singaporean PAP, which was multi-ethnic, majority Chinese, and democratic socialists, and ethnic riots happened (Chew 1987, 128-9).

Lee demanded social reforms in the whole federation, similar to what he had accomplished in Singapore, which angered more conservative UMNO leaders (Frost and Balasingamchow 2009, 414). In addition, there were economic disagreements, since the Malaysian government demanded all investor applications in Singapore for tax-free status to receive approval from it, and rejected many of

---

34 Fong Chong Pik, dubbed "Plen" by Lee Kuan Yew, attacked the PAP thereafter as "soft, bourgeois, English-educated, pleasure-loving middle-class types, beer-swilling, golf-playing, working and sleeping in air-conditioned rooms and travelling in air-conditioned cars" (Lee 1998, 384).

these applications to keep Singapore down (Lee 1998, 600).
With all these disagreements, the Malaysian parliament
voted to remove Singapore from the federation, which came
into force on August 9, 1965 (Chew 1987, 128-9).[35]

Singapore was under significant pressure upon
independence because it had few natural resources, a very
small army, and needed to import its water. On the other
hand, it also had a stable government with a decimated
Communist opposition, and a very well-trained and
educated workforce (Frost and Balasingamchow 2009,
423).

With tough new labor laws, the once restive labor force
became calm, and very few strikes happened after the late-
1960s (ibid., 425). There has been no major union-led strike
since the 1980s. The last major strike activity was in 1986
by the shipping industry. Workers in essential services are
prohibited from striking and are covered under the
Criminal Law Act. Other workers have to report their strike

---

35 Ethnic differences did matter to some extent. Lee quoted Tunku, the
Malaysian prime minister (1957-70), "[Malays] can't do business. They
have no idea how to make money. The Chinese will do the business. They
know how to make money, and from their taxes, we will pay for the
government. But because... the Malays are not very clever and not good at
business, they must be in charge of the government departments, the police
and the army." (Lee 1998, 442). Though Lee himself was not explicitly
racist, he did agree with the sentiment that East Asians, including the
Chinese, were more hard-working and economically prosperous than
Malays and other Southeast Asians. He argued that climate plays an
important role in that East Asians, having survived in colder and more
extreme conditions, have developed more skills and traits like resoluteness,
toughness and innovativeness than Southeast Asians, who have lived in
warm climates, where fewer skills were needed for survival (see Barr
1999). This would explain the success of the Singapore Chinese. On the
other hand, Lee did concede to Deng Xiaoping, who had voiced his doubts
to Lee about China being able to catch up with the rest of the world, that
"we, the Singapore Chinese, were the descendants of landless peasants
from Guangdong and Fujian in South China; whereas the scholars,
Mandarins and literati had stayed and left their progeny in China. There
was nothing that Singapore had done which China could not do, and do
better" (Lee 2000, 645).

14 days ahead of time unless arbitration is ongoing, in which case no strike is permitted. The punishment for participating in illegal industrial action is either a S$2,000 fine or imprisonment for up to six months. Industrial conflict is regulated by the model of tripartism, where the government intervenes between employers and employees (Han 2012).

Welfare policies actually became more restricted after independence with the number of people on welfare rolls declining from over 22,000 in 1966 to less than 7,000 in 1976. The government insisted on family responsibility to take care of the handicapped, weak and poor (Turnbull 2009, 320). Lee argued that welfare undermined the self-reliance of the people (Lee 2000, 104).

In 1967, Lee's government implemented the national draft for all 18-year old males in order to provide the army with soldiers to defend the country, but also to discipline the population, and reduce the likelihood of student protests, boycotts and riots (Frost and Balasingamchow 2009, 427). As a further measure of discipline, Lee also cracked down on newspapers, putting the Eastern Sun, Singapore Herald and Nanyang Siang Pau out of business for allegedly fomenting political unrest in Singapore. Lee told the press, "Freedom of the press, freedom of the news media, must be subordinated to the overriding needs of Singapore, and to the primacy of purpose of an elected government." (ibid., 428).

Lee Kuan Yew and even his son, Lee Hsien Loong, current prime minister, have built up a reputation for suing critics for defamation in order to protect their reputation, or to silence their critics (Situ 2014).[36] Lee defended his tendency for lawsuits by arguing the importance of PAP ministers to remain beyond reproach and maintain

---

36 In one case, Roy Ngerng, a former hospital employee in Singapore, had accused Lee Hsien Loong to have misappropriated CPF funds. Lee subsequently sued Ngerng for defamation of character (described in: Situ 2014).

credibility (Lee 2000, 130-1).

In order to cement their political power, Lee restricted opposition political parties by creating group constituencies in 1988, which generally favored the PAP (Abshire 2011, 151). During the 1960s, Singapore had experienced huge population growth, and the government dis-incentivized having more than two children by canceling maternity leave arrangements for the third child, charging higher hospital fees for the birth of the third child, eliminating tax deductions for the third child, and discriminating against families with three children in government-built housing projects. Increasing educational levels and rising female labor participation have contributed their share in reducing fertility rates (ibid., 140-1).[37]

Lee also noted the cultural problem that many more women are educated, and men did not want to marry their educational equals but preferred wives with less education, and he, therefore, wanted educated women to marry their equals and have two or more children (Lee 2000, 136-7), even though fertility was highest for less educated women (ibid., 140).

During the first years of PAP rule, the main approach of the government was import-substitution industrialization, by which the creation of trade barriers and government incentives for companies would create industries and absorb the unemployed population. But import substitution depended on a strong internal market to absorb all of the products, which was lacking since independence from

---

37 Ironically, the Singaporean government is currently worried about the opposite trend, namely not enough offspring and a shrinking population. The government is currently spending $1.3 billion per year to encourage its citizen to reproduce. Parents get a marriage and parenthood package of $15,000, tax breaks and extended maternity leave, but to no avail. By 2012, the fertility rate was 1.2 per woman (Leyl 2012). The fertility rate hit replacement levels in the mid-1970s, and were further reduced since then. Since the mid-1980s, the government has actively promoted a policy of having more than two children, and it even set up a matchmaking agency to help college graduates find partners (Weathers 2012).

Malaysia.

Since independence, Lee pursued a strategy of export-led industrialization, which heavily relied on foreign funding and attracting foreign talent (Abshire 2011, 134). The government granted huge tax breaks to foreign businesses and investors, and it attracted them via stable labor relations and low strike activity. Decisions with regard to job assignments, promotions and lay-offs were put into the hands of management. But in order to receive workers' approval for this harsh regime, the government supported the creation of the national retirement fund, the Central Provident Fund (CPF) (ibid., 135). The CPF savings were often used to promote housing development projects, and workers could dip into their funds to finance apartments. In addition, the goal of housing policy was to create racially and ethnically integrated housing communities (ibid., 139). For Lee, the CPF-housing scheme was also meant to guarantee industrial peace (since most workers were promised to be able to buy a house with their savings), and to create a politically loyal electorate (Lee 2000, 96-7, 105, 165-6).

In addition to the CPF, which set aside 40% of the worker's wages, the government encouraged workers to set aside additional income in the Post Office Savings Bank, which uses the capital to invest in infrastructure like roads, bridges, airports, power stations, and the mass transit system. The savings were so enormous that the government never had to borrow from foreign funds to finance those projects (ibid., 106). The government prioritized on modernizing the urban landscape by promoting the building of skyscrapers, high-rise flats and and offices (Turnbull 2009, 317). In 1971, the government set up the National Wages Council, in which members from government, management and labor worked together to set wages. The government provided support for vocational and technical training program to build skills in the workforce (Abshire 2011, 135).

To attract more investors, Lee's government also created the Development Bank, which provided partial funding for investor-led projects. It also created state companies, which ran as joint-venture partnerships with foreign corporations (ibid., 135). The creation of those state companies also allowed the government to target growth industries such as transport, shipbuilding, oil refining and others.

When the British had announced their plan to withdraw their bases from Singapore, Lee panicked, because tens of thousands of jobs depended on the British bases, and so he traveled to England and successfully made the case to the British government to allow Singapore to take over the bases and receive financial assistance. Beginning in the 1960s, when increasing oil exploration occurred in Southeast Asia, major oil companies like Mobil and Esso set up refining operations in Singapore. By 1970, oil was 40% of Singapore's manufacturing exports (ibid., 136). With increasing need for shipbuilding and ship repair, Singapore became the most important Asian hub behind Japan. When Bank of America established a "dollar market" in Singapore, which funneled loans to borrowers in Southeast Asia, Singapore became an important financial center (ibid., 137).

Another major pillar of investment stability was the strict stance of PAP against corruption. In 1952, the British had set up the Corrupt Practices Investigation Bureau (CPIB) to fight lower and middle level corruption in the bureaucracy. When PAP came to power, the CPIB was instructed to go after high-level bureaucrats, while lower level bureaucrats were given simpler procedures and clearer guidelines as to what they are allowed to do. In 1960, Lee's government changed the definition of gratuity and corruption to include anything of value. Prosecutors were also permitted to use any proof that the accused was living beyond his means as evidence that he had received a bribe (Lee 2000, 159).

In 1963, it became compulsory for witnesses summoned to CPIB to testify, and in 1989, the maximum corruption fine increased tenfold to S$100,000. False statements led to imprisonment and fines up to S$10,000 and corruption proceeds can be confiscated by the court. High-level ministers had lost office and were imprisoned due to corruption charges (ibid., 160). To keep a clean electoral system, campaign spending was kept low, voting gifts were prohibited, and organizing car rides to the polls on election day were prohibited (ibid., 165). Civil servants and public officials were paid very high salaries to retain talent in the public sector and reduce the incentive for corruption (ibid., 166). In 1995, the Goh Chok Tong government pegged ministerial and senior civil servant salaries to their private sector counterparts (ibid., 169).

These policies paid off, and the economy grew very quickly. There was an economic crisis in the mid-1970s, following the oil embargo from the Middle East, but investments in housing and communications kept down unemployment (Turnbull 2009, 327). A brief economic slowdown in the 1980s was reversed with the attraction of multinational firms to set up their Asia headquarters in Singapore, offering banking, accounting and legal services to clients. In addition, the government took advantage of its Chinese speaking businessmen to serve as intermediaries between China and the English-speaking west. They also aggressively pursued foreign direct investments in China to benefit from their rapid growth as well (Abshire 2011, 148).

The only downside of heavy reliance on foreign investors was the fact that much of the income growth benefited those same investors, while there was little trickle-down for the workers. Between 1959 and the early-1970s, the wages of low wage workers increased by about 5%, while they doubled and tripled for executives (Turnbull 2009, 328).

Lee finally stepped down from office in November 1990, with his chosen successor being Goh Chok Tong (Lee 2000, 671). Lee became a senior minister (1990-2004), and minister mentor (2004-2011) advising the cabinet, after which he became senior adviser to the Government of Singapore Investment Corporation (GIC). Lee has been secretary general of PAP until relinquishing that post to Goh in 1992. He still holds his parliamentary seat in Tanjong Pagar, which he has held since 1955.

Most recently, in 2013, Lee has strongly encouraged Singaporean parents to speak Mandarin with their children, which he considers- along with English- one of the major languages of the future.[38] The "Speak Mandarin" campaign has its roots in 1979, when the government had officially launched this policy. The goal is to convince people to speak less dialect (mainly Hokkien, Cantonese and Hakka), and speak more Mandarin.[39]

Lee Hsien Loong and other Hakka Politicians in Singapore

In 1990 the same year that Lee stepped down from office, his son, Lee Hsien Loong, was appointed deputy prime minister, serving for 14 years in that role before becoming prime minister himself. Loong, as he is called by his father, was born on February 10, 1952, studied at Nanyang Primary school, Catholic High School and National Junior College. He was awarded a scholarship to study mathematics in Trinity College, University of Cambridge in 1971, and three years later graduated first class honours in mathematics and received a diploma in computer science. He received a Master of Public Administration from the Kennedy School of Government in Harvard University in 1980.

Loong joined the Singapore Armed Forces in 1971, and attended the US Army Command and General Staff College in Fort Leavenworth, eventually becoming brigadier-general in 1983. He was discharged the following year to campaign in politics. He became a member of parliament in

---

38 Youtube. "LKY: Speak Mandarin at Home."
  http://www.youtube.com/watch?v=gnlepdMccps
39 Singapore Infopedia. "Speak Mandarin Campaign."
  http://eresources.nlb.gov.sg/infopedia/articles/SIP_2013-07-04_122007.html

1984, and was promptly appointed to be junior minister of trade and industry and defense. He chaired the Economic Committee, advising the government to reduce business costs, reduce corporate/personal taxes and increase consumption taxes to maintain competitiveness.

In 1987, Loong was promoted to minister for trade and industry and second minister for defense; roles which he held until 1992. After surviving cancer in 1992, Loong became chairman of the Monetary Authority of Singapore in 1998, and became finance minister in 2001. Loong became prime minister and PAP leader in 2004, and pushed for a limitation of the work week to five days. He also argued in favor of two month paid maternity leave and financial incentives for mothers with four children to encourage more births.

In 2006, three months before the general elections, Loong had announced a $2.6 billion "progress package" to redistribute budget surplus to Singaporeans, rental and utility rebates for public housing dwellers, pension increases, low-wage worker subsidies, and military members. To be more welcoming to opposition voices, Loong reduced the number of group representation constituencies that favor the PAP, and increase the number of non-constituency members of parliament and nominated members of parliament, which favor the opposition. In 2011, the PAP won re-election, but with fewer votes than in the previous election.[40]

Besides Loong, there are several other Hakkas that made it into political leadership positions. Charles Chong You Fook has been a member of parliament and became its deputy speaker in 2011.[41] Foo Mee Har, who was a

---

40 Lee Hsien Loong's biography is available on the Singapore government website.
http://www.cabinet.gov.sg/content/cabinet/appointments/mr_lee_hsien_loong.html More details on policy can be found in Wikipedia. "Lee Hsien Loong." http://en.wikipedia.org/wiki/Lee_Hsien_Loong
41 Wikipedia, "Charles Chong". http://en.wikipedia.org/wiki/Charles_Chong

businesswoman before joining politics, has been a member of parliament (2011-).[42] Hon Sui Sen was a former finance minister (1970-83).[43] Howe Yoon Chong was a member of parliament (1979-84), defense minister (1979), and health minister (1982-4) who devised Singapore's infrastructural and financial framework, such as the Mass Rapid Transit system, Changi airport and public housing.[44] Richard Hu Tsu Tau was the finance minister (1985-2001), health minister (1985-7) and minister for national development (1992-3) before becoming chairman of the Singaporean property development company Capitaland.[45]

Lai Kew Chai has been the longest serving member of the Supreme Court (1981-2006).[46] Lee Khoon Choy was a journalist (1946-59), and then member of parliament (1959-84), was a diplomat in between and afterward (1968-74, 1984-88), and was an investment consultant after his work in public service.[47] Lee Yi Shyan is a current member of parliament (2006-) and senior minister of state in the ministry of trade and industry (2011-).[48] Lina Loh Woon Lee is a non-constituency member of parliament from the opposition Singapore People's Party (2011-).[49] Josephine Teo Li Min has been a member of parliament (2006-), and senior minister of state in finance and transport (2013-).[50] Yong Nyuk Lin was former minister of education (1959-63), minister of health (1963-8), and minister of communications (1968-75).[51] Yong Pung How served as

42 Wikipedia, "Foo Mee Har". http://en.wikipedia.org/wiki/Foo_Mee_Har
43 Wikipedia, "Hon Sui Sen". http://en.wikipedia.org/wiki/Hon_Sui_Sen
44 Wikipedia, "Howe Yoon Chong".
    http://en.wikipedia.org/wiki/Howe_Yoon_Chong
45 Wikipedia, "Richard Hu". http://en.wikipedia.org/wiki/Richard_Hu
46 Wikipedia, "Lai Kew Chai". http://en.wikipedia.org/wiki/Lai_Kew_Chai
47 Wikipedia, "Lee Khoon Choy".
    http://en.wikipedia.org/wiki/Lee_Khoon_Choy
48 Wikipedia, "Lee Yi Shyan". http://en.wikipedia.org/wiki/Lee_Yi_Shyan
49 Wikipedia, "Lina Loh". http://en.wikipedia.org/wiki/Lina_Loh
50 Wikipedia, "Josephine Teo". http://en.wikipedia.org/wiki/Josephine_Teo
51 Wikipedia, "Yong Nyuk Lin". http://en.wikipedia.org/wiki/Yong_Nyuk_Lin

former chief justice in the Supreme Court (1990-2006).[52]

---

52 Wikipedia, "Yong Pung How".
   http://en.wikipedia.org/wiki/Yong_Pung_How

5: Thailand

The largest group of non-Thai people are the Chinese, who are 15% of the total population. Of the 9 million Chinese, 2.6 million are of Hakka descent (Chan 2010, 162). The largest Chinese group are the Teochews that make up more than half of the Chinese in Thailand, followed by the Hakkas, who dominate in the Nan, Chiang Rai, Phrae and Lampang provinces in the northern region (Schrock et al. 1970, 89-90). The earliest Chinese that traveled to Thailand came in 200 BCE. Migration and settlement in what was known as Siam occurred in the thirteenth century, mainly male traders, who frequently intermarried with local Thai women (Chan 2010, 162).

The offspring of Thai and Chinese mixed relations were called "lokjins", and include many Thai prime minister such as Phibun Songkram, Nai Pridi Phanonomyong, Kukrit Pramoz, Chatichai Choonhavan, Banham Sioparcha, Chuan Leekpai, Thaksin and Yingluck Shinawatra (Lee 2013, 2), the last two are Hakkas from Meixian.[53] Most of the Chinese migrants had arrived between the late nineteenth and the early twentieth century. There has long been a division of labor between the Thai and the Chinese people. Thai's focus on public service and the army, and the Chinese focus on business.

There were many Chinese traders, which put them in a very privileged position. One of the biggest banks, the Thai Farmers bank, is owned by the Lansam's, a Hakka family. In 1995, they were listed as the third wealthiest family in Thailand, owning $2.3 billion (Chan 2010, 162). As an

---

[53] Chinaqw.com.cn. 泰国总理他信：我是华裔客家人. July 1, 2005. http://www.chinaqw.com/news/2005/0701/68/596.shtml. Thaksin Shinawatra is interviewed in this article and says that his Hakka heritage and business character explained his business success. "有一条重要的经验书中没有写出来，那就是客家人经商的良好品德，靠诚信发家。这是我的客家上祖传下的最宝贵遗产。"

entrepreneurial people, in the late-1950s an estimated 70% of Thai Chinese were somehow engaged to trade or commerce (Coughlin 2012, 121).[54] Many Chinese were brought into Thailand as wage laborers by western colonial powers, because they were known for their industriousness (Schrock et al. 1970, 101).

Despite their privileged position, the Chinese were discriminated against by the government. In 1909, the Chinese were forced to adopt Thai names. When king Rama VI came to power in 1910, he accused the Chinese for lack of loyalty to boost Thai nationalism and his own popularity among the Thai. In one of his writings, Rama referred to the Chinese as the "Jews of the Orient". The Chinese in Thailand made a living as tax farmers in the nineteenth century. With the end of the absolute monarchy in 1932, the military took over the country, and many Chinese businessmen lost their royal patronage. They continued to make a living as small-scale entrepreneurs.

With the end of World War II, the military dictatorship stepped up discrimination against the Chinese by heavily taxing Chinese businesses, and using the revenues to subsidize Thai-owned businesses (Chan 2010, 162-3). The Chinese also faced political discrimination: following a 1952 act against communists, hundreds of Chinese, who were accused of being communist were imprisoned (Chaloemtiarana 2007, 156). In addition, the Chinese were barred from 27 different occupations such as bus or taxi drivers (Chan 2010, 162-3).

---

54 Coughlin (2012) describes how keeping the businesses in the hands of the family, loyalty among Chinese employees, lack of opportunities outside of business, lenient Chinese creditors help the Chinese in their enterprise-making. The Thai businessmen tend to be mistrusted by Chinese businessmen, who posess most of the capital, which makes it doubly difficult for the Thai businessmen to succeed (121-4). In addition, there are differences in values, where Chinese are very materialistic, and define their status strictly in terms of business success, while the Thai's Buddhist orientation emphasizes spiritual, non-material goals. Status is derived from relationships with the royalty and the bureaucracy (ibid., 197).

Many trades, which were dominated by the Chinese, were brought under direct government control. But some Chinese businessmen were able to secure themselves continued patronage by paying huge sums to high-ranking Thai officials or military men in return for protection. After the 1972 military coup, the Chinese political privileges ("crony capitalism") were attacked, which forced the ingenious Chinese to expand their business network to the Chinese in the neighboring countries (Chan 2010, 162-3).

As much as the anti-Chinese Phibun regime of the 1930s and 1940s wanted to exclude the Chinese from the business realm by setting up public enterprises, they could not help but to hire Chinese businessmen to head these public firms due to their business know-how (ibid., 167; also discussed in Skinner 1958, 186-7). The Thai government has pursued a policy of ethnic assimilation, which has been fairly successful. All people born in Thailand are granted citizenship, have to adopt Thai names and receive Thai education (Suryadinata 2013, 283).

With the rise of parliamentary democracy in the 1980s, a rising number of Chinese businessmen have entered the political fray. Thailand, besides the Philippines and Singapore (the latter is majority Chinese), allows the Chinese to occupy the highest political offices in Southeast Asia. "Money politics", which involves the deep political influence resulting from Chinese wealth, has been an important part of Thai politics (Chan 2010, 163). What favored Chinese running for high political offices were their increasing economic concentration and their perceived security of holding wealth (Siamwalla 1980).

Many Chinese businessmen also joined the government in order to ensure and increase their property holdings (Girling 1996, 36). Chinese financiers generally recoup their investments in political campaigns through government projects (Chan 2010, 164). With the rise of businessmen politicians, the traditional client-patron relationship between businessman and politicians was severed, leading to a complete business domination over Thai politics (Pathmanand 1998, 2001).

Thaksin Shinawatra

One among the successful Hakka Chinese businessman, who made it as prime minister of Thailand, was Thaksin Shinawatra. Most of the business elite are Teochew Chinese with Hakka businessmen falling outside that Teochew circle (Van den Broek 2012). Thaksin is a billionaire, who started out as a police officer, and acquired his riches by gaining monopoly rights over mobile phone networks through contracts with government organizations (Terwiel 2011, 287).

Thaksin's paternal great-grandfather was Seng Sae Khu (Khu Chun Seng), who was a Hakka Chinese, who migrated from Guangdong to Siam in the late-1860s. He married a local Thai girl named Thongdi, and became a tax farmer, which was a popular occupation among Chinese migrants. The government auctioned the right to tax farmers to collect taxes on goods and services, and they were allowed to keep a portion of the tax. One profitable domain in tax collection revolved around gambling, opium and liquor, which were heavily consumed by the Thai Chinese (Phongpaichit and Baker 2009, 26).

After staying in Bangkok, Seng moved to Chiang Mai in 1908 (ibid., 27). His eldest son Chiang Sae Khu was Thaksin's grandfather, who married Saeng Somna, another Thai woman, and the daughter of Nai Mun Somna, a big landowner, trader and village headman, and the couple helped out Saeng in the caravan trade (ibid., 29). The family imported plain silk from Burma, then dyed it, and re-exported it to Burma as sarongs. Chiang developed the idea to improve cotton cloth and sell it, which was a huge business success, as the profits were reinvested to buy land (ibid., 31-32; Prani 1980, 199-203).

In 1932, Chiang built a factory in Sankamphaeng, which

weaved, dyed and tailored silk clothes (Plaior 1987, 53-4).
The twelve children of Chiang and Saeng helped out in the
family business, though the sons received higher education
first (including Thaksin's father, the second-born son Loet),
while the daughters went into the trade (Phongpaichit and
Baker 2009, 32). The eldest son, Sak, became a general in
the Thai army, and so did his children (ibid., 34). The
younger children were all able to be sent abroad to gain
skills in the silk business, because the family became
prosperous enough (ibid., 32). The family kept their
Chinese name (Khu) until 1938, when Chiang's eldest son,
Sak, decided to rename the family Shinawatra (Jitra 2004).
In order to improve the position of the Shinawatra family,
many of its members married into powerful Thai dynasties,
such that by the 1950s it became an established commercial
family in Chiang Mai (Phongpaichit and Baker 2009, 33;
Prani 1980, 182-6).

Loet Shinawatra, Thaksin's father, was born in 1919, and
studied at Thammasat University, but only for one term,
because he was needed in the family business (Phongpaichit
and Baker 2009, 34-5). He married Yindi Ramingwong, a
native Hakka from Meixian.[55] Loet was destined to become
the inheritor of the Shinawatra company, but he declined,
and opened up a small coffee shop instead. Loet's brother,
Sujet, became a property developer and municipal councilor
in Chiang Mai, and gave Loet a job as head of the loan
department. Using the contacts he acquired from there,
Loet began to purchase two cinema houses, a bus service, a
motorcycle agency, a BMW dealership, a gas station, and
several tracts of land. Using his wealth as a base, Loet
joined politics and became a MP in Chiang Mai in 1969. But
the military coup led to the dissolution of parliament in
1971, which was not re-installed until 1975, when Loet
returned as MP (ibid., 35-6). A year later Loet stepped down
from office after having been cheated of his fortune (Ariwat

---

55 China Daily. "Thai PM Seeks out Roots in Meizhou." July 4.
    http://www.chinadaily.com.cn/english/doc/2005-07/04/content_456688.htm

2003, 91).

But Loet's temporary financial problems did not impede
the great education that Thaksin was able to receive.
Thaksin was born on July 26, 1949, and attended Monfort
College, one of Chiang Mai's most established, prestigious
and expensive primary and secondary schools
(Phongpaichit and Baker 2009, 36). Thaksin decided to
enroll in the police academy, where he enjoyed the physical
training, camaraderie and discipline (ibid., 37).

After graduating at the top of his class, he received a
scholarship to pursue MA studies in criminal justice in
Eastern Kentucky University. Upon his return, he was
assigned into a police guard unit, being the secretary of
Loet's friend Prida Patthanathabut, who became
government minister in 1975. Prida lost his position the
following year, and so Thaksin was assigned to a regular
police station in Bangkok. Then he married Pojaman
Damaphong, the daughter of Bangkok police commander
Samoe Damaphong (ibid., 38-9). After a row with his
father-in-law, Thaksin used a scholarship to get his PhD in
criminal justice in Sam Houston State University in Texas.
Upon his return, Thaksin was assigned to various police
departments and taught in police educational institutions.
On the side he unsuccessfully tried to run a cinema
business, which he sold off at a loss (ibid., 40).

Commercial success came with the business leasing of
IBM computers to government offices in 1981. Five years
later he won a bid to implement a plan to equip the police
departments with computers (ibid., 41; Sorakon 1993, 36-
7).[56] Thaksin also opened a cable TV service, and got the
Bangkok authority to license a radio broadcasting system
for the public buses, and the police authority to license a
pager system for officers to make SOS calls (ibid., 43).
Thaksin won paging and mobile concessions from another
firm, and the demand for the mobile phones was really

---

56 The fact that his father-in-law was head of the Bangkok police department
   certainly helped him get the deal approved.

high, such that his profits rose to 3 billion baht in 1995. Out of 22 telecom concessions from 1988 to 1991, Thaksin won seven of them. What helped him win these concessions were his good relationships with government ministers, who also granted his company a contract to install 3 million landlines (ibid., 44-5).[57]

In 1994, Thaksin expanded his mobile phone concession to include new digital technology, and expanded cable TV services to neighboring Laos and Cambodia. He then won mobile phone concessions in Laos, Cambodia, the Philippines and India. He bought 10% of shares into the Bangkok Expressway Consortium, which built and managed the freeways in Bangkok. Because his business was so successful, he brought them into the stock market, taking advantage of the liberal capital inflows of the early-1990s. In 1994, the total revenues of Thaksin's companies were 25 billion baht, and the asset value was 56 billion baht (US$ 2.4 billion) (ibid., 49).

With the military beginning to recede into the background, and more businessmen joining active politics, Thaksin used his superior position in the telecom business and his political networks to launch his own political career. In 1994, Thaksin was appointed foreign minister of the Phalang Tham Party (ibid., 53). Thaksin hoped that with himself in government, and his friend and banker, Vichit Suraphongchai, being appointed communications minister, he would be able to receive more government concessions for his mobile phone network business. After the 1995 elections, where Thaksin was the party leader, he became appointed deputy prime minister, and that enabled him to expand his phone concession by another five years, and reduce revenue-sharing with the government, so that his own revenue share increased. After the 1997 elections, his party was reduced to one seat and was ejected from the

---

57 As one of Thaksin's supporters said, "Thaksin knows lots of people [and] has no problem dealing with senior officials, because he knows how to show respect." (Sorakon 1993, 83-4).

government (ibid., 54-5).

When the Asian financial crisis happened, wiping out many businesses as foreign creditors pulled their capital out of Thailand following the baht devaluation, Thaksin came out almost unharmed. The reason was that his friend, Thanong Bidaya, was finance minister at that time, and a week before the baht devaluation was announced by the government, Thanong had leaked the information to Thaksin, allowing him enough time to hedge against the devaluation. His favorable financial position allowed him to acquire other companies, raise money on the stock market, and grow his business further (ibid., 58-9).

His business success motivated him to re-enter politics. He argued that due to new trends in technology and free trade Thailand needed to weaken the factionalism that is so common in politics, and replace it with an efficient management style to make the country globally competitive (Shinawatra 1999, 230-1). He launched his own Thai Rak Thai Party (TRT) in 1998, inviting former Phalang Tham politicians, property developers, academics, former and current officials to join the party (Phongpaichit and Baker 2009, 64-5). During the election campaigns, he portrayed himself as a defender of small and medium enterprises and received much electoral support from it (ibid., 77). In addition, as a result of rural farm protest demanding debt relief after the devastating financial crisis, Thaksin made himself a champion of the rural poor by promoting a debt moratorium, a generous loan program for farmers, and a low-cost health insurance scheme for farmers (ibid., 81-2).

Thaksin's electoral strategy worked, and in 2001 his TRT received 248 of the 500 parliamentary seats with most of his support coming from the north and northeast of the country (ibid., 89). After swallowing up the New Aspiration Party in early 2002, TRT commanded 296 seats, and together with two other smaller coalition partners, Thaksin had a comfortable 364 seat majority in parliament (ibid., 95). Thaksin's goal in office was to promote the growth of the economy (ibid., 100). Part of the "Thaksinomics" strategy was to promote mass manufacturing, foreign direct investment, and foreign exchange, and strengthen local enterprises to raise the domestic consumption share in the economy, and reduce reliance on export (Looney 2004, 71).

Thaksin fulfilled his campaign promise and declared a moratorium on farmers' debt payments. His government brought small loans to street vendors through the Government Savings Bank (GSB). It set up a spending package for families of retired civil servants, who passed away. It created a village fund, which are one million baht loans given to each villager with the intention of raising productivity and starting new businesses (ibid., 72-3).

In practice, however, the government did not closely track how the village fund was spent, and did not care too much how to recoup it. As a result, a major portion of the funds were used by villagers to pay off old debts and to finance consumption, which increased consumption in the economy (Phongpaichit and Baker 2009, 108)[58] Nonetheless, export remained an important part of the Thai economy, which had benefited from strong demand from a rapidly growing China, and rising world prices for Thai agricultural products (ibid., 127). Thaksin also used his time in office to give his own business a $600 million tax break (Terwiel 2011, 290).

To strengthen small businesses, Thaksin promoted the creation of an SME bank to steer credit to small and medium-size businesses. The One Tambon (district) project was meant to modernize the production and distribution process of small firms. His government supported housing projects for state workers and low income people, and advanced the privatization of state enterprises. In 2003, the government put in place a capital creation scheme, whereby various assets were reclassified in order to allow owners to use them to get access to capital.

---

58 Preferably, the consumption went to mobile phones and cable TV, which benefited Thaksin's company (see Phongpaichit and Baker 2009, 264).

Thaksin also prioritized large infrastructural projects, e.g. develop Chiang Mai as international aviation hub, transform Pyhuket into a high-tech research and development hub, and build a canal through Thailand to shorten shipping routes (Looney 2004, 73-6). Thaksin also wanted to reflate the property market, which had crashed after the 1997 financial crisis, and promoted preferential interest rates to developers and home buyers (Phongpaichit and Baker 2009, 111).

To bolster rural, popular support, Thaksin's government created a cheap life insurance scheme, cheap housing, cheap computers and television, subsidies for buying taxis, and loans to buy bicycles (ibid., 107). To pay for these programs, Thaksin took out funds from state financial institutions, and privatized state firms. Yet the privatization particularly benefited Thaksin's and government officials' friends (ibid., 119-20).

Just like many other Thai governments before him, Thaksin tried to restrict the activities of NGO's and independent groups. He instructed the foreign ministry to persuade foreign sponsors of Thai NGO's to withdraw funding (ibid., 144). NGOs were subjected to bureaucratic harassment, and rules for monthly reports on activities and finance were more strictly enforced. Visa standards for foreigners were toughened (UN 2004).

Thaksin also restricted media freedom by taking on a controlling stake in TV news media, firing or transferring critical reporters and journalists, changing media content to include more entertainment and less political news, filling the broadcasting regulatory body with political allies, and demands by Thaksin to reduce negative news coverage (Phongpaichit and Baker 2009, 149-51). Journalists in the newspapers received intimidating chats with government officials, nice facilities as a way to produce compliance, threats of removal for non-compliant reporting, and interference and micromanagement of news content (ibid., 152). Thaksin operated an anti drug war, which led to the death of 2,500 people (Cropley 2006).

To solidify government power, Thaksin took advantage of the 1997 constitution which increased executive power and centralized power in his political party, receiving funds from big business. He made politicized appointments of senior bureaucrats, and strengthened the role of the military, while at the same time tying them to the government via patronage. The provincial governors were brought under closer control of the central government (Phongpaichit and Baker 2009, 196).

During his 2005 reelection campaign, Thaksin toured the north and northeastern part of the country, where his principal voter base was. He made many populist promises, including an extension of the village fund, lower taxes and more loan schemes for rural farmers (ibid., 232). That was an unusual strategy in Thai politics, since the other parties did not court the rural vote as intensely. As part of his electoral strategy, he attacked the old privileges of establishment bureaucrats, intellectuals, opposition Democratic Party politicians, and old-status families, and wanted the popular vote in order to rule with few democratic restrictions (ibid., 234).

The reelection strategy worked, and TRT received 377 of the 500 seats in parliament, while the opposition Democrats received a mere 96 seats (ibid., 237). Ironically, Thaksin's blatant populism was one cause of his undoing, because he created antagonism among the conservative politicians and the military, who invoked the monarchy to challenge the Thaksin government (ibid., 259).

In January 2006, Thaksin's family sold the Shinawatra Corporation for 73.3 billion baht (US$ 1.7 billion), and paid no taxes on it (ibid., 261). When this information became public, the angered opposition politicians under the leadership of Sondhi Limthonkul and PAD (People's Alliance for Democracy; an organization founded to topple Thaksin) used this incident as a justification to call for Thaksin's resignation (ibid., 267). PAD was a formidable opposition, which gained its backing from the middle class, royalists and the military (ibid., 270). Under increasing pressure, Thaksin called for snap elections in February 2006, and gained 56% of the votes, down from 61%, but still with a comfortable majority (ibid., 271-3).

The administrative court then suspended the election rerun, and the attorney general called for the dissolution of the TRT and the Democrats due to malpractice. Another election was scheduled for October 2006 (ibid., 276). The month before on September, Thaksin traveled to New York to give a speech in front of the UN, but learned that the military under general Sonthi Boonyaratklin rolled out the tanks in Bangkok to topple the Thaksin government in a coup d'etat (ibid., 282-3). The goal of the generals was to get rid of Thaksin, imprison him, and destroy his support base (ibid., 289).

Thaksin disappeared into exile in London (ibid., 293). In May 2007, the constitutional tribunal dissolved TRT, and banned many of its leaders from serving in politics for five years (ibid., 297). But the party reconstituted itself under a different name, first as People Power Party (PPP) (ibid., 307), which was again dissolved three months later in December 2008.[59] Later the Pheu Thai Party (PTP) was founded.[60] The military hoped that by carrying out the coup, they could permanently remove Thaksin's influence, but to their disappointment, Thaksin's voter base remained loyal to him, and gave his party another comfortable majority in the 2007 elections (Phongpaichit and Baker 2009, 315).

Samak Sundaravej, a Thaksin loyalist, became prime minister, and returned Thaksin's revoked passport, which allowed him to return from exile (ibid., 317). But only a few months later, he fled the country again to London, as the

59 AFP Bangkok. "Thai Premier Banned from Politics, Ruling Party Dissolved: Court." December 1, 2008.

60 Nation. "Puea Thai Party to Elect Leader on Sunday." December 3, 2008. http://www.nationmultimedia.com/home/Puea-Thai-Party-to-elect-leader-on-Sunday-30090122.html

Supreme Court sentenced Thaksin in a majority vote to two years in jail for abuse of power (ibid., 329-30). The UK withdrew Thaksin's visa following the court sentence, and Thaksin then fled to Dubai (ibid., 336). The PTP held itself in power for a few more months, this time under the helm of Somchai Wongsawat, Thaksin's brother-in-law.

The opposition against PTP, and the pro-Thaksin forces increased, and after defection of several government coalition parties, the Democrat Abhisit Vejjajiva was voted in as prime minister, serving from 2008 to 2011 (ibid., 343). Abhisit is another Thai politician of Hakka Chinese descent, and his background will be treated briefly.

Abhisit Vejjajiva

Abhisit was born on August 3, 1964 to an elite family from Bangkok. His father was a Sino-Thai Hakka, and his mother was Thai (Lee 2013, 51). Abhisit's paternal ancestors came from China via northern Vietnam. His great-grandfather, Phra Bamrad Naradura, or Long Vejjajiva, was a health minister in Thailand. A hospital in Nonthaburi was named after him. The family name Vejjajiva was granted by King Rama VI, which translates as "medical profession" (Tumcharoen 2009). Abhisit's father was in government too, and served as deputy minister of health.

Abhisit received a bachelor's degree in philosophy, politics and economics in Oxford University. He received a master's degree in economics there as well. After teaching in the Chulachumklao Royal Academy and the economics department of Thammasat University of Thailand, he launched his political career in 1992, being elected to parliament for the Bangkok district. He then became Democratic Party spokesman, deputy secretary of the prime minister, and government spokesman. Under prime minister Chuan Leekpai, he was minister of the prime minister's office. After the electoral defeat of the Democrats in 2005, he was elected party leader, and played opposition until 2008, when he was able to cobble together a governing majority. The Democratic Party's main electoral base was the urban population in Bangkok and the middle class in southern Thailand, who are very much opposed to Thaksin's populism (Lee 2013, 51-3).[61]

Once Abhisit's Democrats were in power, they were themselves besieged by the so-called "red shirts", or pro-Thaksin people from north and north-east Thailand. They are funded by Thaksin and his friends, and have organized huge street protests in Bangkok against the Abhisit government in 2010, leading to heavy-handed police and army crackdowns and the death of scores of red shirt protesters (Buncombe 2014). Abhisit pushed for many populist policies himself, once in power in the hope of receiving the popular vote that was loyal to Thaksin, but failed (Liu 2014; Hewison 2013, 185-6). In the 2011 parliamentary elections, the Pheu Thai Party led by Thaksin's youngest sister, Yingluck Shinawatra, gained the majority of votes, allowing her to become prime minister for three years.

Yingluck Shinawatra

Yingluck is the youngest child of Loet Shinawatra and Yindi Ramingwong, and was born on June 21, 1967. She attended the Regina Coeli College, a private girl's school, followed by Yupparak College, a co-educational secondary school. She received a bachelor's degree in political science and public administration in Chiang Mai University in 1988, and a master's of public administration in Kentucky State University in 1991, the same university that Thaksin

61 On a side note, Abhisit's wife, Pimpen, is a distant relative of Potjaman Damapong, the ex-wife of Thaksin. New Mandela. "The Shinawatra Family Tree." August 8, 2011. http://asiapacific.anu.edu.au/newmandala/2011/08/08/the-shinawatra-family-tree/

used to attend.[62]

After her studies, she became a marketing and sales intern at Shinawatra Directories Co. Ltd., a telephone directory business. She was promoted to director of operations. In 1994, she became the general manager and later deputy CEO of Rainbow Media, a subsidiary of International Broadcasting Corporation. In 2002, she became CEO of Advanced Info Service, Thailand's largest mobile phone operator. She resigned from that position after the 2006 sale of the Shinawatra Corporation, which owned it. She was accused of being complicit in avoiding to pay taxes on the shares she held with the Shinawatra Corporation, though no formal charges were brought against her. She then became the managing director of SC Asset Co. Ltd., the Shinawatra family property development company. In late-2008, Yingluck was asked to lead the Pheu Thai Party, but she declined, and stayed on as a leading party member.[63]

In February 2009, Thaksin appointed Yingluck to oversee the center region of the party organization in the country. After many defections from his non-relative allies, Thaksin became really suspicious of outsiders, and had said that he only trusted his own family members with important positions. Subsequently, his sister Yaowapha ran the north, his brother Payhap the northeast, and his sister Yaowares the south (Phongpaichit and Baker 2009, 344).

When Yongyuth Whichaidit, former health minister under Thaksin and head of PTP, announced his resignation

---

62 In an interview, Thaksin said that he himself sent Yingluck to college in the US. He explained that because their mother died when Yingluck was very young, he took very good care of Yingluck, and also helped her get started in his business. He said of her that "[w]e have the same way of thinking, the same DNA." Thilo Thielke. "Thailand Must be United Again." Spiegel International, June 15, 2011.
http://www.spiegel.de/international/world/spiegel-interview-with-thaksin-shinawatra-thailand-must-be-united-again-a-768492.html

63 Samui Times. "Who Is Yingluck Shinawatra."
http://www.samuitimes.com/yingluck-shinawatra/

before the 2011 elections, Thaksin and Yingluck agreed that she should become the party leader, and contest the elections to become prime minister. Thaksin said of his sister, "some said she is my nominee, but that is not true. But it can be said that Yingluck is my clone, another important things is that Ms. Yingluck is my sister and she can make decisions for me, she can say yes and no on my behalf." PTP promptly won the next elections with 265 of the 500 seats, and a governing majority of 296 MP's made Yingluck prime minister.[64] Yingluck held herself in office for 3 years. After long protests by the opposition, she dissolved parliament and called out snap elections in February 2014.[65] She continued as a caretaker prime minister until the constitutional court ousted her in May 2014, citing an illegal transfer of a senior official and graft during the rice pledging scheme.[66] Her successor was the then-minister of commerce Niwatthamrong Boonsongpaisan, who was himself ousted by the military only two weeks after taking on premiership. Army general Prayuth Chan-ocha appointed himself as the new prime minister on May 22, 2014, and has run the country under martial law ever since.[67]

---

64 Ibid.
65 Krishnadev Calamur. "Thai Prime Minister Dissolves Parliament, Calls New Elections." NPR, December 9, 2013. http://www.npr.org/blogs/thetwo-way/2013/12/09/249729649/thai-prime-minister-dissolves-parliament-calls-new-elections
66 The Nation. "Ousted Yingluck to Face Impeachment over Rice Pledging Scheme." May 8, 2014. http://www.nationmultimedia.com/politics/Ousted-Yingluck-to-face-impeachment-over-rice-pled-30233176.html
67 Lindsay Murdoch. "How the Military Seized Control in Thailand." Sydney Morning Herald, May 23, 2014. http://www.smh.com.au/world/how-the-military-seized-control-in-thailand-20140523-zrlkw.html

6: Philippines

There are about 1.5 million Chinese in the Philippines, making up about 2% of the total population. Only a small portion of those Chinese, an estimated 10,000, are Hakka, with most of them coming from Fujian province (Chan 2010, 150-1). The large-scale immigration of Chinese to the Philippines goes back to the late-1500s[68], when Spain colonized the islands and attracted many Chinese to come. Many of the Chinese, however, were subjected to harsh treatment, which was followed by insurrections, which was followed by killing and massacring from the colonial masters. Therefore, the number of Chinese that came to the Philippines fluctuated, but newcomers kept on replenishing the Chinese population despite the many deaths (Guerrero 1966, 25).

The Chinese were fairly independent from the main society, remaining concentrated in their ghettos, preserving their cultural tradition, while refusing to adopt local customs, while being interested in economic and commercial contacts with the Spaniards and the native Filipinos (ibid., 28).

Despite native fears of the Chinese, they were essential to the country, because they were the craftsmen and retailers, which the Spaniards and Filipinos did not want to be. They also bribed the Spanish Royal officials to ensure favorable treatment. As a result, the Chinese occupied a middle position in society, somewhere between the ruling Spaniards and the mostly lower class Filipinos.

Ethnic segregation continued until the nineteenth century, when a mixed (mestizo) population among the three groups was created. The common combination would usually be Chinese men and Filipina women, and Chinese women and Spanish men. The Chinese who intermarried

---

68 It should be noted that the first migrants arrived in the tenth century, and commercial relations developed in the twelfth century (Suarez 1999, 48)

with Filipinos often took on native customs and names, though in other families Chinese traditions prevailed (Bernal 1966, 64-5). Chinese mestizo children were not considered Chinese, which allowed them the freedom to buy, sell and own land. But the mestizo children received Chinese credit and their father's sense of business, such that they became middlemen and moneylenders (Seagrave 1988, 9).

As middlemen, the Chinese distributed imported goods to the provinces, and then collected goods from the provinces to be sold to companies for foreign export (Chu 2010, 94). Despite some setbacks[69], the Chinese also became successful moneylenders. They took advantage of the Filipino's tendency to celebrate great feasts on borrowed money from the Chinese, using their own land as collateral. When the Filipinos were unable to repay the loan, their land was seized, which happened quite frequently, and so the Chinese mestizos came to own more and more land (Seagrave 1988, 9).

The next business opportunity for Chinese mestizos came when the Americans held the Philippines as a colony after the 1898 war with Spain. The Americans had purchased the haciendas, that were previously owned by the Spaniards, and re-sold them at 8% interest to the local Filipinos. The Filipinos, of course, lacked the capital, and had to resort to Chinese mestizo moneylenders again, resulting in default and land forfeiture. The tenancy rate of Filipinos was higher under American rule than under Spanish rule (ibid., 13).[70] Ironically, the Americans pursued a segregationist race policy and discouraged the long practice of miscegenation

---

69 Occasionally, the moneylenders would not get repaid, see Chu (2010, 101).

70 As Alfonso Felix Jr. (1966) unsentimentally put it, "For four hundred years our [Filipino] officials have exploited the Chinese and for four hundred years the Chinese have recouped their losses by exploiting us. For generations, the Chinese and ourselves have held each other in mutual contempt. We expect no ethics from them and they expect us to behave like savages." (4-5)

among Filipinos and Chinese people (Chu 2010, 332).

This fairly exploitative relationship resulted in the formation of a powerful oligarchy. 400 millionaire families controlled 90% of the national wealth. The sugar export delivered a huge windfall to the sugar barons, and the Chinese financiers benefited too. Among the billionaire families, Ferdinand Marcos, former president (1965-86) and a Chinese mestizo, ranked as the sixth richest. Other provincial dynasties consisting of Chinese mestizos included the Laurels in Batangas, the Aquinos and Cojuangcos in Tarlac (out of which a Hakka Chinese and mestizo, Corazon Aquino née Cojuangco, served as president from 1986 to 1992), the Quirinos and Crisologos in Olocos Sur and the Lopezes in Visayas (Seagrave 1988, 13-4).

Under the rule of Ferdinand Marcos, the Chinese business community was harnessed for Marcos' political goals. He used the Federation, a chamber of commerce established in 1954 and consisting of Chinese businessmen, to exert political control over the Chinese, and receive financial and political support from them. Marcos promised political protection for Chinese businessmen in return for financial patronage (Carino 1998, 48). Marcos used $168 million and patronage to win his 1969 re-election, and aside from using business money, he used up the foreign currency reserves, which led to an IMF bailout and austerity policies that reduced the standard of living of the Filipinos in half (Seagrave 1988, 218-9).[71]

In the mean time, protection of the Chinese was clearly necessary due to the disproportionate number of kidnappings of Chinese people (ibid., 117), which reached a

---

71 Of course, Marcos also used his power for personal enrichment, which came from his tobacco monopoly, import license fees for personal profit, company kickbacks, gambling proceeds, US government aid, World Bank and IMF funds, business confiscation, landgrabbing, and diamond and gold possession (Seagrave 1988, 296-7). An estimated $10 billion were looted from the Philippine treasury during his 21-year rule (Hunt 2013).

record high in 1997 (Hau 2014, 137). The point of kidnapping Chinese business people was to collect ransom for the perpetrators, who were either domestic rebel groups, who complained about not being paid by the government, or Chinese drug and kidnapping syndicates from mainland China, Hong Kong and Taiwan (ibid., 144-5). In the most recent years thanks to more education and remittances, there has been an increase in the service sector and the middle class. Chinese entrepreneurs were also able to claim control over conglomerates, which were the sole domain of the mestizo elite. It was in large parts made possible by a 1975 law, which granted citizenship rights to Filipino Chinese (Shiraishi 2014, 82).

In spite of the economic dominance of the Chinese and mestizos, there were a group of other Chinese in the Philippines that have helped in the development of the Filipino leftist movement (Hau 2014, 174). In 1927, Chinese Filipino communists founded the Philippine Chinese Labor Association (PCLA), and made ties with the Filipino-based Congreso Obrero de Filipinas (COF) worker federation (ibid., 175). Of the 35 founding members of the Philippine Communist Party, 3 of them were Chinese. During the Japanese occupation in World War II, Chinese in the Philippines founded a guerrilla group called Wha Chi to fend off the occupiers, but they were severely marginalized during the Cold War era by an anti-communist government (ibid., 176).

One of those communists was the poet and essayist Du Ai (pen name of Cap Chuanmei), who is a Hakka from Dapu County in Guangdong, who did liaison work for the communist party in Manila during the Japanese occupation (ibid., 180), and used his fighting experiences in the Philippines in his writings (ibid., 182). In the next section, I examine the life of a famous Hakka descendant, Corazon Aquino.

Corazon Aquino

Corazon Cojuangco Aquino was the first female president of the Philippines (1986-92), and came to power after the assassination of her husband and long-time politician Benigno "Ninoy" Aquino in 1983 and the fall of then-president Ferdinand Marcos after the elections of 1986 (Buss 1987, 1-2). Being the wife of a powerful opposition political leader, and a member of the social elite have certainly helped her to become president (Richter 1991, 528).

Some scholars celebrate her as a great president, who "made a fresh start in bringing back democracy, reviving the economy, reforming the military, suppressing rebellion, countering the communist insurgents, and restoring the Philippines to its honored place in the family of nations" (Buss 1987, 1). Others see her impact more mixed, because "she had made little headway in improving the quality of life of her people. The democratic institutions she struggled to rebuild remained flawed and weak. Corruption prevailed, and Filipinos were increasingly cynical about the state of their nation" (Reid and Guerrero 1995, 2). In addition, "[d]espite populist rhetoric, her roots were in the elite, and her sentiments lay with the conservative Catholic hierarchy and their reformist allies in business, academia, and the professions", which led her to carry out a "style of politics based on patronage and personality, even at the expense of the spirit of her people power promises" (ibid., 110).

Corazon Aquino was born on January 25, 1933 into one of the 400 families that controlled the economy of the Philippines.[72] Despite her portrayal in the international

---

72 Even to this day, "large numbers of peasants remain impoverished tenants on farmland owned by members of the upper and middle classes. Others work for low wages as seasonal agricultural labors." Further, while other countries like Japan, South Korea and Taiwan have produced prosperous farmers via land redistribution reforms due to US pressure, no such reforms had been implemented in the Philippines, such that extreme inequality had

media as a "champion of the impoverished masses", she came from a Chinese mestizo elite, which had attained economic privilege via land-holdings and tariff-sheltered industries. Her parents were Jose "Don Pepe" Cojuangco and Demetria Sumulong. Don Pepe was a senator and member of the house of representatives, and Aquino's maternal grandfather, Juan Sumulong, served as a senator. Aquino's great-grandfather, Xu Yu Huan came from Hong Hian in Fujian province, China in 1861, and hispanicized his name to Jose Cojuangco (ibid., 10-11).

Aquino's Chinese ancestors were Hakkas (Christiansen 1998, 1; Mathari 2008; Diaz 2009). The Cojuangco's move toward fortune happened when Aquino's great-aunt Ysidra (daughter of Jose Cojuangco) became the mistress of General Antonio Luna. Luna made himself an enemy of his supreme commander and was sentenced to death upon which Luna gave all his gold to Ysidra, which she used as a starting capital for her family's business. The Cojuangco's established a freight business, which became very successful (Reid and Guerrero 1995, 11). Jose Cojuangco had three children with Antera Estrella, who descended from a wealthy family from Malolos, Bulacan. The children were Ysidra, Melecio and Trinidad. Melecio became a politician and was elected to the national assembly in 1907. His wife was Tecla Chichioco, and his four children were Jose "Pepe" (Aquino's father), Juan, Antonio and Eduardo "Endeng". The Cojuangco's owned sugar mills, stock brokering firm, and became the largest landowners in Central Luzon. Together with the Jacinto and Rufino families, they founded the Philippine Bank of Commerce (Diaz 2009).

Ironically, this economic and political success of the Cojuangco family soon turned into family-internal feud in the political arena. Melecio's oldest son Pepe was a legislator. His daughter Corazon Aquino- the archenemy of Ferdinand Marcos, whose regime was associated with the

---

remained a central feature of life in the Philippines (Lande 2001, 101).

death of her husband- became president, and Aquino's son, Benigno III, or "Noynoy", became president as well after serving as Congressman and senator, serving in that post since 2010. Melecio's youngest son Endeng, whose wife was Josephine Murphy, had six children, including Eduardo "Danding" Jr., Mercedes, Aurora, Ismael, Enrique "Henry", and Manuel. Danding became a congressman and governor of Tarlac.

Danding bought up many companies and became a close friend and beneficiary of Ferdinand Marcos, such that he was able to control $1.5 billion in assets through this government connection. After the overthrow of Marcos, Danding followed him to the US, but he returned to the Philippines and ran for president in 1992 after founding his party the People's Coalition. Endeng's other child, Mercedes, had married Gilberto Teodoro Sr., who was an administrator of Social Security during the Marcos regime. Their child, Gilbert Jr., became the presidential candidate in 2010, and lost against his third cousin Benigno III (Diaz 2009).

Corazon Aquino went to a Roman Catholic convent school in Manila, but her family relocated to the US in 1946, where Aquino studied in Raven Hill Academy in Philadelphia and Notre Dame Convent School in New York. After that she studied in the College of Mount St. Vincent in the Bronx, and received a degree in French and mathematics. She returned to the Philippines in 1953, where she became a law student in Far Eastern University, which was owned by Cojuangco and three other families (Reid and Guerrero 1995, 14). Aquino wanted to attend the University of the Philippines, but was refused to go there, because her father was the chair of the board of trustees at Far Eastern University.[73] Only a year later, Aquino dropped

---

73 "Essential Cory Aquino: The Young Cory." Ninoy and Cory Aquino Foundation.
http://www.coryaquino.ph/index.php/essential/article/4a66ceac-f098-11df-b3cf-001617d76479

out of law school to marry Benigno "Ninoy" Aquino, the son
of Benigno Aquino Sr., who was another powerful person in
the Tarlac clan. While Ninoy was very sociable and
politically ambitious, Corazon was more reserved and did
not like to associate with strangers (Reid and Guerrero
1995, 14).

The couple had five children, including Maria Elena,
Aurora Corazon, Benigno III ("Noynoy"), Victoria Elisa and
Kristina Bernadette. Ninoy was a reporter for Manila Times
and a presidential adviser, before being elected as a mayor
of his hometown Concepcion at age 22 (1955). Four years
later, he became the vice governor of Tarlac, and in 1961 he
became the governor of Tarlac. In 1967, Ninoy became
senator, the only vocal opposition elected to the Senate to
the Marcos regime. Ninoy wanted to take over the
presidency and oust Marcos, so he ran for president in 1973.
Marcos was not eligible to run again due to the two term
limit, but on September 21, 1972, Marcos declared martial
law, and made sure to imprison his political opponents
including Ninoy, who then spent several years in jail.[74]

Confined to his prison, Ninoy staged hunger strikes that
severely harmed his health. In 1977, the court sentenced
him to death, but Marcos refused to carry it out, fearing
international condemnation (Reid and Guerrero 1995, 18).
Three years later, Ninoy suffered from a heart attack, so
Marcos relented and allowed him and his family to go to
exile in the US, and to undergo a heart surgery. Ninoy was
given a fellowship to study in Harvard (ibid., 19), and later
MIT. Though Corazon was very happy with this
arrangement, Ninoy became very restless, and wanted to
return to the Philippines to challenge Marcos once more.[75]
Ninoy returned to the Philippines in August 1983, and was

---

74 "Essential Cory Aquino: Her Life with Ninoy Aquino." Ninoy and Cory
   Aquino Foundation.
   http://www.coryaquino.ph/index.php/essential/article/516835d2-f099-11df-
   b3cf-001617d76479
75 "Essential Cory Aquino: Her Life with Ninoy Aquino." op. Cit.

presumably assassinated by Rolando Galman in the Manila airport on the tarmac. It was not until Aquino herself became president that she was able to have the courts prosecute 16 soldiers and sentence them to life imprisonment for murder (Reid and Guerrero 1995, 19-20).

From that moment on, Corazon Aquino began to step into politics. The opposition to Marcos decided that Aquino would be the most qualified candidate to win the next presidential elections, because she was considered "the only candidate capable of uniting the opposition". The opposition "needed a candidate with a reputation for personal integrity who could appeal to conservative oppositionists, left-leaning progressives, ...the broad masses", and "a candidate acceptable to Washington" (ibid., 23). After initial reluctance, Aquino decided to run for presidency (ibid., 23-4). The elections were set in 1987, but the US and other international creditors pushed Marcos to call snap elections in 1986.

The elections on February 7, 1986, were fraught with bribery, coercion, stealing of ballot boxes, and counting manipulation. But in this election, the middle class, business community and the Catholic church, that each usually did not get involved in politics, strongly supported Aquino, and really wanted to get Marcos out of power, and so they guarded the ballot.[76] Mostly female computer programmers, who were pressured by their superiors to falsify the election results to benefit Marcos decided to walk off the job (Reid and Guerrero 1995, 25). So the election commission declared Marcos the winner of the elections (ibid., 26).

As a result, several reformist generals in the army led by defense minister Johnny Enrile plotted a coup against Marcos. But Marcos' supporters uncovered the plan, and

---

76 "Essential Cory Aquino: The Unpaved Road to the Presidency." Ninoy and Cory Aquino Foundation.
http://www.coryaquino.ph/index.php/essential/article/9921a3da-f1f3-11df-b3cf-001617d76479

moved to arrest Enrile and his supporters. But a large number of Filipinos, who opposed the Marcos regime, came to the square and formed a human shield against Marcos loyalists. With many Aquino supporters now on the streets, the pressure for Marcos to resign was enormous, which he promptly was forced to do on February 25, when Aquino was sworn in as president.[77] Ironically, immediately after Aquino's oath of office, Marcos repeated the same exercise for himself. But since the US no longer gave him any backing, he fled to exile to Hawaii, where he died in 1989 (Reid and Guerrero 1995, 32).

Aquino's challenges in office were enormous. The Philippines were facing $28 billion in foreign debt, rampant poverty, Communist insurgency, Muslim secession movements, dysfunctional infrastructure and schools, and an underpaid labor force (ibid., 34). Aquino had run on a platform of removing Marcos and restoring democracy and people's power (ibid., 37), which was very popular in a country replete with extreme wealth inequality (ibid., 35), yet she appointed conservatives to the most powerful posts, who resisted any great political changes (ibid., 40).

Aquino also appointed liberal human rights advocates into her cabinet, which revealed that she was in favor of respecting human rights, but on fiscal issues she sided with conservative businessmen (ibid., 41). Aquino, who was determined to pay off the national debt and maintain credibility with investors[78], ensured the repayment of $4 billion in foreign debt, but throughout her tenure the national debt still increased by $9 billion to reach $30 billion.[79] But debt to GNP ratio decreased from 93.7% in 1986 to 66% in 1991 (Estanislao 1992, 43). 40% of the country's revenue at the beginning of the Aquino administration went to debt service (Reid and Guerrero 1995, 119).

---

77 "Essential Cory Aquino: The Unpaved Road to the Presidency." op. Cit.
78 "Essential Cory Aquino: The Unpaved Road to the Presidency." op. Cit.
79 New York Times, "Manila Plan to Cut Debt". February 21, 1992.

There was a lot of political infighting in Aquino's cabinet.[80] Because the labor minister Augusto Sanchez was a communist, and because Aquino empowered cabinet members rather than centralize tasks in her own office, the cabinet meetings became highly contentious, which the thereafter free press covered in detail. One of the essential problems of the administration was that Aquino was considered more a referee rather than a micromanaging leader, which was a problem in the Philippines, which is a strongly personality- rather than institution-based society (Reid and Guerrero 1995, 41-2).

Another line of conflict was between the fairly conservative military and the liberal lawyer, Joker Arroyo, an important presidential adviser to Aquino, who was seen as being close to the detested communists (ibid., 47, 50). Arroyo himself was forced out in September 1987 (ibid., 141) The communists and the anti-Marcos forces were in a coalition during the Marcos rule (ibid., 51).[81] Aquino herself was willing to negotiate with communist leaders to achieve a cease-fire and an end to local uprisings, though as a devout Catholic she was no supporter of godless communism (Reid and Guerrero 1995, 76). The communists waned, and no longer became a threat against her administration by the end of her term (ibid., 245).

---

80 As former president, Francisco Nemenzo, put it in an interview, "The economic ministers are controlled mostly by what I call the Makati Mafia, but the ministries that are concerned with relations with the masses, like social work and labour, are handled by those I would consider to be progressive... it is a very well-balanced cabinet. The trouble is that since class interests are rather contradictory a balanced cabinet may not be a lasting cabinet." (Rajaretnam 1986, 126).

81 It should be noted that Marcos had brutally repressed the communist insurgency. By the time he was ousted, they made up 16,000 guerrilla fighters. Marcos with the heavy support of the US expanded the armed forces to over 200,000 soldiers to crack down on the communist fighters. Joel M. Reyes and Rodolfo Sosonto Perez III. "The Philippines under Ferdinand Marcos", n.d., AN Online Guide about the Philippine History. http://www.oocities.org/collegepark/pool/1644/marcosera.html The Communists in the Philippines have been scrutinized by Sison (1986)

In order to reduce revolutionary sentiments among the impoverished peasantry, the Aquino administration tried to pursue agrarian reforms to redistribute land to poor farmers, but that initiative stalled due to political infighting and conservative opposition (ibid., 116). In 1988, Congress finally passed the Comprehensive Agrarian Reform Program, which stipulated the land sale of wealthy owners and the break-up of the large farms, but in reality landowners got away by being only required to sell stocks of land to peasants, while effectively continuing to control the estate.

Aquino was fairly reluctant to strictly enforce her new policy, because many of her own family members were large landowners. Her brothers Pedro and Peping opposed any kind of land reform, and so the government dropped the case for acquiring the Cojuangco's (Aquino) family property. When Jose "Linggoy" Alcuaz, a high-ranking government official tasked to break up the telephone monopoly controlled by Aquino's cousin, stepped forward and raised this problem with Aquino herself, Aquino covered her ears with her hands. Linggoy lost his job soon thereafter due to pressure to resign (ibid., 154-7).

Aquino's main priority priority was to restore democracy (Shiraishi 2014, 81), disband the parliament filled with Marcos loyalists, set up a revolutionary government, and appointed a commission to draft a new constitution, which was approved the following year.[82] 80% of all registered voters cast their ballot, and 70% approved of the new constitution (Reid and Guerrero 1995, 104). In the new Congress, Aquino received confirmation for her popular mandate by receiving 22 of the 24 senate seats, and a large majority in the house of Representatives.

As a sign of rift within the cabinet, Aquino fired her defense minister Enrile in November 1986. Aquino survived several assassination attempts against her, which were

---

82 "Essential Cory Aquino: The Unpaved Road to the Presidency." op. Cit.

organized by rebellious soldiers.[83] In one instance, Aquino had to call for US support to repel the rebels that almost took over government (Reid and Guerrero 1995, 165-6)[84]. 99 people were killed and 570 were wounded (ibid., 171).

The coup against Aquino, while not getting rid of her, undermined economic development, because it frightened foreign investors and businesses from making investments (ibid., 140). It also undermined any of her other reform efforts, since governing became a matter of mere survival (ibid., 171). During Aquino's rule, GDP increased by 3.5% in 1986, 4.3% in 1987, and 6.7% in 1988. But in the last few years of her administration, the country experienced a series of earthquakes and volcano eruptions, six coup d'etat attempts and periods of power shortage. Other important parts of her economic agenda were the liberalization of foreign investment restrictions, agrarian reform, and privatization of government corporations.[85]

After only one term, Aquino decided not to run for re-election following the one-term limit specified in the 1987 constitution, and her chosen successor Fidel Ramos became her successor as president in 1992.[86] Aquino died on July 31, 2009 due to heart failure and colon cancer (Drogin and Gliona 2009).

Benigno Simeon "Noynoy" Aquino III

Corazon and Benigno II ("Ninoy") Aquino's son, Benigno "Noynoy" Aquino III grew up to become the president of the Philippines himself. He attended Ateneo de Manila University, and received a bachelor's degree in economics.

---

83 "Essential Cory Aquino: The Unpaved Road to the Presidency." op. Cit.
84 The US did not bomb rebel positions, but they sent war planes on patrol to scare the rebels.
85 Encycloperia of the Nations, "Philippines: Overview of Economy", http://www.nationsencyclopedia.com/economies/Asia-and-the-Pacific/Philippines-OVERVIEW-OF-ECONOMY.html#ixzz0clOAibWu
86 "Essential Cory Aquino: The Unpaved Road to the Presidency." op. Cit.

After his graduation, he moved to Boston with his family. After his father, Ninoy, was assassinated, Noynoy returned to the Philippines with the rest of his family. He worked for Philippine Business for Social Progress and Nike Philippines. When his mother became president, he became the vice president of the family-owned Best Security Agency Corporation.[87]

During one of the coup attempts against Corazon Aquino's government, he was seriously wounded because he stood in the line of fire. He was hit by five bullets, one of which still is in his body.[88] In 1993, he switched to another family-owned business, which was a sugar refinery. In 1998, he joined politics as a member of the Liberal Party, serving three terms (9 years) as a member of the House of Representatives and deputy speaker between 2004 and 2006. In 2006, Noynoy was appointed vice-chairman of the Liberal Party, and in 2007, he became a senator. Only one month after the death of his mother, Noynoy announced to run for president in September 2009. He won the elections with a handsome majority on May 10, 2010, and has been president ever since.[89]

Noynoy has been running on a popular platform of eradicating corruption, which has led to high opinion poll ratings, and an upgrade of investor ratings of the Philippines. However, his reform-mindedness is diminished due to the institutional feature of patronage, whereby political support from legislators for his programs can only be generated with the help of appointments and funds. At the same time important social issues like a lack of job growth despite a growing economy, very high rates of

87 Encyclopedia Britannica, Academic Edition. "Benigno Aquino III." http://www.britannica.com/EBchecked/topic/1689897/Benigno-Aquino-III
88 Planetizen Post, "Short Biography: Noynoy Aquino", June 12, 2010. http://planetizen1network.wordpress.com/2010/06/12/short-biography-noynoy-aquino-%E2%80%93-by%C2%A0vonowen/
89 Encyclopedia Britannica, Academic Edition. "Benigno Aquino III." http://www.britannica.com/EBchecked/topic/1689897/Benigno-Aquino-III

poverty, a reduction in manufacturing activity, and a rise in inequality have not been solved thus far (Thompson 2014, 452). Besides alleviating poverty, the government will have to deal with a shrinking agricultural sector by opening up employment opportunities and provide a good education to people (Shiraishi 2014, 83).

7: Guyana

Guyana is the only country in this study that is not located in Asia, but in South America, bordering Suriname, Brazil and Venezuela. The original inhabitants were the Arawaks, a peaceful tribe of hunters, fishermen and cultivators. By the fifteenth century, they were later replaced by the violent, warrior-like Caribs. When the Spanish explorers came to South America, they found the Arawaks easier to conquer than the Caribs, who defended themselves ferociously against the invaders (Merill 1992, 4). The first European settlers to Guyana were the Dutch, who came in 1616, and they colonized it.

The Dutch West India Company put up agricultural, sugar and tobacco plantations, but found that the indigenous labor was unreliable to work it, so they turned to African slaves (ibid., 6), which later led to slave rebellions. By the mid-1700s, the Dutch allowed many British immigrants to come in, and they soon constituted the majority of the settlers (ibid., 7). The Dutch came into increasing conflict with the British planters, because the former had imposed huge taxes on the latter, and a document was drafted to reform the constitution, and give the planters more rights. It was called the Concept Plan of Redress. During the Napoleonic wars, France occupied Netherlands in 1795, and the British exploited the opportunity to occupy the Dutch colonies in South America the following year (ibid., 8).

In 1831, Berbice and the United Colony of Demerara and Essequibo were unified under British Guyana. British rule lasted until 1966, when the country became independent. In 1838, slavery was abolished, and many Afro-Guyanese former slaves banded together in communities to grow and sell their own food, which threatened the British planter elite (ibid., 9). In addition, the planters now faced a significant labor shortage, which they attempted to fill by attracting Portuguese immigrants. But they concentrated on the retail trade, and disliked plantation labor. The British planter elite now turned to the Chinese. Between 1853 and 1912, Guyana pulled in 14,000 Chinese, who were themselves also very restless, and joined the retail trade whenever they could, and so they pulled in Indian laborers as well (ibid., 10).

The Chinese indentured workers were required to work for five years on the plantations before they could change their occupation. Many Chinese, including Hakkas from the southern provinces of China, chose to stay after the contract was over. Many Guyanese Chinese turned to colonial civil service, or low-skilled jobs, which include hairdressing, to make a living. After 1879, the Chinese came in as free immigrants at their own expense. Initially, there were very few Chinese women, but since the 1860s, many women also entered the country.[90] Many descendants of the indentured servants from China chose to completely assimilate, and the Chinese language, customs and kinship organizations disappeared. There was significant intermarriage with East Indians and Africans. As of July 2009, there were about 2,200 Hakkas in a population of about 770,000 (Chan 2010, 185-6). Following a 2002 census, 43.5% of Guyanese people were of East Indian descent, 30.2% were black African, 16.7% mixed, 9.1% Amerindian, and 0.5% other.[91]

Due to political pressure during World War I, the British government outlawed indentured servitude in 1917 (Merill 1992, 13). The economy diversified to include bauxite and rice production. The Great Depression of the 1930s hurt all segments of society, particularly the workers (ibid., 14).

---

90 The British wanted to have Chinese women migrate to ensure the reproduction of Chinese laborers over the long term. The Hakkas were preferred migrants, because of their industrious and adventurous reputation; the fact that women did not bind their feet, which made them useful for plantation labor; and their large-scale conversion to Christianity, which made them capable of being integrated. See Sue-A-Quan (2000).

91 CIA World Fact Book. Guyana.
https://www.cia.gov/library/publications/the-world-factbook/geos/gy.html

In the aftermath of World War II, Britain granted more political rights to the Guyanese people, which led to the development of political parties (ibid., 15). The left-wing, Marxist PPP (People's Progressive Party) became the leading party, and was divided in two factions, mainly along ethnic lines. Forbes Burnham, an Afro-Guyanese led the one faction, and Cheddi Jagan, Indo-Guyanese, led the other faction. When Jagan became prime minister in 1953, the British became alarmed about his radical program and sent in troops to topple Jagan's administration (ibid., 19).

In the mean time, the ethnic tensions within the PPP increased, leading the ambitious Burnham to found his own party, the People's National Congress (PNC), in 1958 (ibid., 20). His time in power came in 1964, when prime minister Jagan, who was restored to power in 1961, faced huge labor strikes, and after the elections, when Burnham's left-wing PNC agreed on a coalition government with the conservative, business-oriented United Force (UF), which included the ethnic voice of the Chinese, Amerindians and Portuguese as well (ibid., 21-22).

Burnham was forced to moderate course and allowed foreign investors and industries to enter the country. He negotiated the formal independence from Britain (ibid., 23). But after the 1968 elections, the PNC gained the absolute majority in parliament, and allowed Burnham to shift more toward left-wing policies, such as supporting the creation of cooperatives. Burnham continued to exploit racial differences to gain the loyalty of the middle-class blacks, who would otherwise have supported more traditionally capitalist policies (ibid., 24). Burnham consolidated his power position, and when the constitution changed in 1980 to make the largely ceremonial president a powerful chief executive, Burnham promptly became president only to die five years later in office (ibid., 25-6).

After his defeat in 1964, Cheddi Jagan only played a marginal political role, but when Burnham successor Desmond Hoyte opened up the political process, Jagan's

PPP won the 1992 elections, making him the president until his death in 1997. By the 1990s, Jagan had moderated his course, and no longer spoke of a revolution, but welcomed pro-market reforms.[92] As of currently, the president is Donald Ramotar, and the prime minister Sam Hinds, both from the PPP. Hinds has incontinuously served as prime minister since 1992 with the backing of Jagan.

Arthur Chung

Amid the ethnically divided country, a politically independent Guyanese of Hakka Chinese descent, Arthur Chung, became the first president of Guyana, serving from 1970 to 1980. Chung was born on January 10, 1918 in Windsor Forest, Guyana to Joseph Chung, a Chinese immigrant and foreman at the Martha Funk-Kee-Fung's rice plantation, and Lucy, an immigrant from Trinidad. Being an Anglican, Chung was baptized at St Jude's Anglican Church in Blankenburg. He attended Windsor Forest and Blankenburg primary schools located on the west coast, and the Modern High School in Georgetown, receiving Junior and Senior Cambridge certificates in 1938.

Chung started his career as a surveyor in the Lands and Mines department, becoming a land surveyor in 1940 and an assistant hydrographic surveyor a little later. He helped dredge the Demerara river. He accumulated his savings to afford his studies in Britain. In 1945 he studied law in Middle Temple, Inns of Court in London. Two years later he became a barrister and worked as an assistant legal examiner in the British civil service. He returned to Guyana in 1948, and practiced as a lawyer before taking up several judge positions. He became an acting magistrate in 1953[93], and a senior magistrate in 1960. One year later he became a

---

92 People's Progressive Party. "History of PPP." http://www.ppp-civic.org/history/historyppp.htm

93 Stabroeknews.com. "Obituary- Arthur Chung." June 29, 2008. http://www.stabroeknews.com/2008/features/06/29/obituary-arthur-chung/#

registrar of deeds of the Supreme court, and the year after Puisne Judge, and the year after Appellate judge.[94]

Being unassuming and unpretentious made him a desired candidate for the presidency, which was newly created in 1970. The position of the presidency was endowed with ceremonial functions with the real power vested in the hands of then-prime minister Forbes Burnham, despite the fact that the president had the formal power to appoint and remove the prime minister and other government ministers. The president was also the commander-in-chief of the armed forces.

But Chung acted with the self-restraint of a trained civil servant, and avoided the political controversies of the 1970s. During his inaugural address, Chung said that "[o]ur survival as a nation will depend on how well we work together." He wanted the people of Guyana to stop quarreling with each other and use the resources to the advantage of all people. Chung's main task was to establish formal and strategic economic relations with other Caribbean and socialist countries. He made foreign trips to the United Kingdom, Antigua, Grenada, Jamaica, India, People's Republic of China, North Korea and Yugoslavia. Chung was confirmed in his office by parliament in 1976, and voluntarily stepped down in 1980.[95] Chung died at the age of 90 in 2008 in his Bel Air Springs home, and left behind a wife (Dorothy), two children, and five grandchildren. His children and grand children live in England.[96]

---

94 Kaieteur News. "Guyana's First President Dies at 90." June 24, 2008. http://www.kaieteurnewsonline.com/2008/06/24/guyana%E2%80%99s-first-president-dies-at-90/

95 Stabroeknews.com. "Obituary- Arthur Chung." June 29, 2008.

96 Stabroeknews.com. "Guyana's First President Arthur Chung Dies." June 24, 2008. http://www.stabroeknews.com/2008/archives/06/24/guyana%E2%80%99s-first-president-arthur-chung-dies/

Conclusion

The extraordinary contributions, which Hakkas have provided in the political sphere in East and Southeast Asia and South America, may best be explained in terms of the unique social pressures that Hakkas were exposed to in Chinese history. As late-coming migrants in Guangdong and Fujian, they were facing poor soils on hill land, and had to be very resourceful, and needed a great degree of internal social coherence and solidarity. There have principally been two escape routes out of poverty: entry into officialdom via the passage of the rigorous civil service examination, and emigration. In either case, the extraordinarily hard work that the Hakkas have put in to improve their economic prospects has also helped some Hakkas to gain access to very high political offices inside and outside China. Examining the lives and circumstances of these Hakka leaders was the content of this study.

What many of the Hakka political leaders in this study have in common is their initial position as outsiders, who fight their way into the political arena. Wherever a Hakka came to lead the country, the Hakka people were the minority of the population, even in countries that were predominantly ethnically Chinese, like in Taiwan or Singapore.

Within China, Hong Xiuqian, a disappointed scholar official candidate, channeled the anger of other disappointed scholar literati against the ruling Qing dynasty, and organized a revolutionary movement that- despite its failure- precipitated the later demise of the Qing dynasty. Deng Xiaoping, a Sichuan Hakka, played a very marginal role in his youth, working in French factories and struggling to make a living. When he joined the Communist party, he climbed his way to the top, but was held back and repeatedly removed by Mao Zedong and his loyalists. It was only after Mao's death, that Deng could become the unquestioned leader of his country, carrying out the economic reforms that have made China so prosperous in the present era. In Taiwan, Lee Teng-hui was not a naturally gifted politician, but a trained agricultural economist and academic. It was after president Chiang Ching-kuo had tapped Lee for his expertise to join government office, that he devoted himself to become a political leader and lead Taiwan into a democracy.

In Singapore, Lee Kuan Yew did come from a rather affluent family, but as many other Singaporeans, his family had suffered economic hardship during the Japanese occupation of Singapore. Singapore had long been a British colony, being ruled directly by British leaders. During Lee's early days as a lawyer, it was not clear whether he would become a politician, but when he was successful in representing the interests of grieving workers, he received the necessary political support to found his party and become the country's first prime minister after independence from Britain. Lee became an outsider when he gave his speeches in the other dialects, Hokkien and Mandarin, to convince his Chinese Singaporean voters to join the Malaysian Federation. He became another outsider when he in vain pleaded in fluent Malay to make Malaysia more meritocratic and less Malay-centered. This eloquent performance sealed Tunku's decision to eject Singapore out of the Malaysian Federation. Singapore has become the role model for rapid economic development and a politically disciplined society, following the Singaporean discourse for the need of "survival", Lee's administration has gone out of its way to attract foreign workers and foreign investments, making it the richest state per capita in Southeast Asia.

In Thailand, Thaksin Shinawatra belongs to a wealthy, Chiang Mai based Hakka business family. This condition was certainly an advantage to Thaksin, but he was the first in his family to accrue billions of dollars thanks to monopoly rights and government concessions. The Shinawatra clan was also not deeply connected to the

Teochew Chinese business community, which dominated Thai commercial life. He joined politics during a time when many businessmen felt it was necessary to do so in order to avoid losing out commercially. But unlike his political competitors, Thaksin grasped the importance of electoral and populist politics, making himself the champion of the poor with many loan and health care schemes to benefit the rural poor in Thailand. This electoral strategy guaranteed popular support for him, making him prime minister, but also made him a pariah among the middle class, the military, the royalists and some businessmen. He was forcibly removed by the military in 2006. The return of his faction to power was accomplished by the premiership of his younger sister Yingluck in 2011, who herself was removed from power in May 2014.

In the Philippines, Corazon Aquino was the wealthy heir of a Hakka-Chinese mestizo family of large landowners, who had wielded significant power and influence in the country. The Chinese businessmen and merchants were politically rather peripheral despite their relative commercial success in the moneylending and trading business, but the Chinese mestizos like the Cojuangcos were able to become economically and politically central. Aquino herself was a political outsider, because she was very unpolitical. She was a devoted housewife and mother. Her husband was the politician, Ninoy Aquino, who was a promising candidate for replacing Ferdinand Marcos until Ninoy was assassinated. The circumstances of Ninoy's death triggered an anti-Marcos political movement, which catapulted Corazon Aquino to political power. She claimed herself to be a direct representative of "people's power". Unlike in Thailand, however, the pro-poor policies were significantly moderated due to the many coup attempts against her rule, the political infighting among various diametrically opposed political factions, and her own privileged class position. Despite the promise of sweeping land reforms to benefit the poor peasants, many exceptions were made to exclude her own family members and close friends. Despite these setbacks a middle class was still able to arise.

In Guyana, the son of a foreman of Hakka heritage, Arthur Chung, made his way through the civil service and the judiciary to gain a high reputation among other political leaders, which made him become the first president of Guyana. In a country that was divided by heavy inter-ethnic conflicts, primarily between people of Indian and African descent, Chung posed as a neutral figure, who quietly administered the country, and built diplomatic ties with other socialist states. The Chinese in Guyana make up a very small minority, and have not as strongly intervened in the political process as in the Asian countries, but a few of them, like Chung, were capable of occupying important positions.

The study of Hakka political leaders can be extended to investigate what factors may explain the tremendous economic and political achievement of other communities that were in the minority. The Jews are a commercially successful group, and though they only make up a relatively small minority of the total US population they are overrepresented among senators and Congressmen in the US. The limitation of this study is the lack of applicability to all other ethnic groups, and future research can consider a comparison with other and similar groups.

The huge question that hangs over the future of Hakka studies concerns the future existence of Hakka political leaders, especially within the context of the declining use of the Hakka language. In a highly globalized world, only the major languages like English, Spanish or Mandarin have the possibility to survive and be widely used over the long term. There may be some efforts to more widely implement TV shows like Hakka TV or course offerings of Hakka in schools and universities, but I doubt that these efforts will stem the general trend toward a decline of Hakka use. In that case, it would be hard to trace back whether somebody is really a Hakka, who is competing for political leadership positions. In the two major Hakka bastions in Mainland China and Taiwan, many of the leaders with Hakka ancestors are not proficient in their own dialect, and would be indistinguishable from political leaders of other dialect groups. One may still find among the leaders with Hakka ancestors that there is a greater proclivity for participating in politics than for other groups, but it would, in any case, be harder to talk and write about it as a "Hakka-thing" per se.

Since Hakka has long been a minority language, there has never been a point to use one's own identity and language group as a way to craft electoral advantage, and lay claim on political power. In fact, overly emphasizing Hakka identity could alienate other ethnic groups, and reduce the likelihood of attaining power. That is acutely true in Chinese minority countries like in Thailand and the Philippines. In that case posing as an ethnically neutral candidate is the most desirable practical agenda for leading a country politically. In fact, none of the leaders that I had studied had a particular inclination toward the Hakka, and instead followed the refrain of uniting all parts of the country and overcome ethnic differences at least on a political level.

What makes the study of Hakka leaders particularly interesting is the fact that there are only very few top leadership positions in each country, and so breaking into the political system is by no means an easy and assured process. The Chinese diaspora has long been known for its very strong entrepreneurial bend, which is why one may be able to see many different Chinese restaurants in all parts of the world where there are Chinese people. Of course, it takes effort and perseverance in order to succeed in running a business just as with politics. But the process of breaking into the political field is fraught with greater difficulty for a minority group, because while entrepreneurial success at a most basic level implies individual effort, specifically for small business owners, politics inherently means establishing strong and many relationships and networks.

For that matter, one might be able to compare big business, which also requires extensive relationship networks for continued success, with politics, and in cases like in Thailand, there certainly is a very strong connection between these two sectors. But here, again, there is a very fine and important distinction between owning a big business and being involved in politics. In the former, one is well-known within the networks and is largely accountable to these networks, which may include business partners, senior government officials, shareholders and clients. Politicians in the highest of all leadership positions on the other hand are very well-known across all sectors of society. The media is hanging all over them, punishing them for any utterance that they will presumably regret. Even in the more authoritarian societies that I studied leaders are the most likely ones to be scrutinized by academics, which is reflected in the many biographies that I had read, and were an essential source material for my study. For that reason, politicians and other important public figures are under much greater pressures to perform well and to act as expected.

While many Hakkas may restrict themselves to the business route, some of them, who harbor a desire to join politics, whether it is for just for personal gain or for public service, do think it is important to become a political leader despite all the external obstacles that the group as a whole may have experienced due to nativism, a complicated political history, or outsider status in society. Time can only tell whether numerous Hakkas will still hold onto power in the future, and whether more countries will be willing to have a Hakka run their country.

Appendix

Summary Table of Hakka Political Leaders

Country (est. Hakka population)	Person (time of reign)	Political position	Social class background	Outsider position
China (35 million[97] or 2.6% of total)	Hong Xiuquan (1851-64)	Revolutionary leader, Taiping Rebellion	Poor family in Guangdong	1.Born in Poverty 2.Failed civil service exam four times 3.Conversion to Christianity (minority belief) 4.Led rebellion against ruling Qing dynasty
China	Deng Xiaoping (1978-1992)	Various: Vice Premier (1975-6, 1977-80), Chairman of CPPCC National Commi	Father was mid-level landowner in Sichuan	1.Worked in France in a factory at half of Frenchmen's wage 2.Victim of two purges carried out by Mao Zedong and his allies (Jiang Qing, Lin Biao etc.) during the Cultural Revolution 3.Following the purge he did manual labor

97 Joshua Project, "Hakka in China".
http://joshuaproject.net/people_groups/12054/CH

		ttee (1978-83), Chairman of CPC Central Military Commission (1981-89), Chairman of Central Advisory Commission of the Communist Party (1981-87).		4.Eschewed titles and the formal top position (e.g. president)
Taiwan (3.5 million or 15% of total population)	Lee Teng-hui (1988-2000)	President of ROC (Republic of China)	Father was small landlord and manager at the local irrigation	1.Was among the few Taiwanese students in high school dominated by Japanese, and had to study very hard 2.A trained agricultural economist called

			service in Sanchih[98]	for public service by Chiang Ching-kuo 3.Opened up Kuomintang to non-Mainlanders
Singapore (250,000 or 4.6% of total population)	Lee Kuan Yew (1959-90)	Prime minister	English-educated, wealthy family with business; paternal grandfather was managing a ship company, investments in rubber and sugar trade; maternal grandfather	1.Turned to black market to survive during hardship of Japanese occupation 2.Initially campaigned on behalf of British politician/lawyer rather than running himself 3.Had to learn Mandarin and Hokkien to convince Chinese Singaporeans to join the Malaysian Federation 4.Had to convince Malaysian leaders (in vain) to become more meritocratic and less Malay-centric 5.Pushed Singaporean development based on "survival" narrative

98 Your Dictionary. "Lee Teng-hui Facts."
   http://biography.yourdictionary.com/lee-teng-hui

			was rubber and property investor	
Thailand (2.6 million or 3.9% of total population)	Thaksin Shinawatra (2001-06)	Prime minister	Wealthy family in Chiang Mai; family businesses include tax farming, silk (historical), property development and politics	1.Began his career as a police officer 2.Teochew businessmen dominate; Hakkas play smaller role 3.To gain majority popular support, he pushed for populist policies, which alienated conservatives 4.Overthrown by military coup d'etat.
Philippines (10,000 or 0.01% of total population)	Corazon Aquino (1986-92)	President	Elite wealthy Chinese mestizo family in Tarlac, Luzon; family	1.No inclination to become a politician before Ninoy Aquino's assassination 2.Initially, little chance of success against Ferdinand Marcos regime in

			membe rs were politici ans, large landow ners, and owned sugar mills, stock broker firm and a bank	elections if people were not mobilized enough 3.During her reign, many political factions in government and coup attempts made governance and reform difficult 4.No inclination to hold onto power and stepped down after one term
Guyana (2200 or 0.3% of total populati on)	Arthur Chung (1970-80)	Preside nt	Father was forema n in rice plantati on, middle class	1.Began his career as surveyor and had to save money to afford law school 2.Avoided heated political confrontation between Indo- and Afro-Guyanese 3.Retained his self-restrained civil service mentality during his entire tenure as president

References

Abshire, Jean E. 2011. *The History of Singapore*. Santa Barbara, CA: Greenwood.

Ariwat, Sapphaithun. 2003. *Trakun Chinnawat [The Shinawatra family]*. Bangkok: Wannasat.

Baum, Richard. 1994. *Buying Mao: Chinese Politics in the Age of Deng Xiaoping*. Princeton, NJ: Princeton University Press.

Barr, Michael. 1999. "Lee Kuan Yew: Race, Culture and Genes." *Journal of Contemporary Asia* 29(2): 145-166. http://unpan1.un.org/intradoc/groups/public/documents/apci ty/unpan004070.pdf

Bernal, Rafael. 1966. "The Chinese Colony in Manila, 1570-1770." In *The Chinese in the Philippines*, Volume 1, edited by Alfonso Felix Jr., 40-66. Manila, Philippines: Solidaridad Publishing House.

Bohr, P. Richard. 2012. "Did the Hakka Save China? Ethnicity, Identity, and Minority Status in China's Modern Transformation." *Headwaters: : The Faculty Journal of the College of Saint Benedict and Saint John's University* 26: 10-18. http://digitalcommons.csbsju.edu/cgi/viewcontent.cgi? article=1013&context=headwaters

Buncombe, Andrew. 2014. "Thailand Protests: Meet the 'Red Shirts', the pro-government Shinawatra Supporters of the North." *Independent*, February 6. http://www.independent.co.uk/news/world/asia/thailand-protests-meet-the-red-shirts-the-progovernment-shinawatra-supporters-of-the-north-9112857.html

Buss, Claude A. 1987. *Cory Aquino and the People of the Philippines*. Stanford, CA: Stanford Alumni Association.

Carino, Theresa Chong. 1998. *Chinese Big Business in the Philippines: Political Leadership and Change*. Singapore: Times Academic Press.

Chaloemtiarana, Thak. 2007. *Thailand: The Politics of Despotic Paternalism*. Ithaca, NY: Cornell Southeast Asia Program Publications.

Chan, Clement. 2010. *Hakkas Worldwide*. Gentilly, Moka, Mauritius: DCI Studios.

Chang, Mau-kuei. 1994. "Toward an Understanding of the Sheng-chi Wen-ti in Taiwan. Focusing on Changes after Political Liberalization." In *Ethnicity in Taiwan. Social, Historical and Cultural Perspectives*, 93-150. Chen Chung-min, Chuang Ying-chang and Huang Shu-min (eds.). Taipei: Institute of Ethnology, Academia Sinica.

Chen, Christine. 2014. "Workers Brave Rain to March against Low Pay on Labor Day." *Focus Taiwan*, May 1. http://focustaiwan.tw/news/asoc/201405010036.aspx

Chen, Jieming, Houfeng Zheng, Jin-Xin Bei, Liangdan Sun, Wei-hua Jia, Tao li, Furen Zhang, Mark Seielstad, Yi-Xin Zeng, Xuejun Zhang, and Jianjun Liu. 2009. "Genetic Structure of the Han Chinese Population Revealed by Genome-wide SNP Variation." *American Journal of Human Genetics* 85(6): 775-785.

Chew, Sock Foon. 1987. *Ethnicity and Nationality in Singapore.* Athens, OH: Center for International Studies, Ohio University.

Christiansen, Flemming. 1998. "Hakka: the Politics of Global Ethnic Identity Building." Spirit: Albord University. http://vbn.aau.dk/files/40334846/No5SpiritDiscussionPaper_Flemming_Christiansen_.pdf

Chu, Richard T. 2010. *Chinese and Chinese Mestizos of Manila: Family, Identity, and Culture, 1860s-1930s.* Leiden, NL: Brill.

Copper, John F. 2013. *Taiwan: Nation-State or Province?* Boulder, CO: Westview Press.

Coughlin, Richard J. 2012 [1959]. *Double Identity: The Chinese in Modern Thailand.* Bangkok: White Lotus.

Cropley, Ed. 2006. "A Populist Billionaire, Thaksin Ruffled a Feather Too Many." *Sydney Morning Herald*, September 21. http://www.smh.com.au/news/world/a-populist-billionaire-thaksin-ruffled-a-feather-too-many/2006/09/20/1158431784671.html

Deng, Maomao. 1995. *Deng Xiaoping: My Father.* New York: Basic Books.

Deng, Xiaoping. 1987. *Fundamental Issues in Present-Day China.* Beijing: Foreign Languages Press.

Diaz, Perry. 2009. "The Cojuangco Wars." *Filipino Journal*, September 4. http://archive.today/hB5FY

Drogin, Bob, and John M. Glionna. 2009. "Corazon Aquino Dies at 76; Restored Democracy to the Philippines." *Los Angeles Times*, August 1. http://www.latimes.com/la-me-aquino1-2009aug01-story.html#page=1

Erbaugh, Mary S. 1992. "The Secret History of the Hakkas: The Chinese Revolution as a Hakka Enterprise." *China Quarterly* 132: 937-968.

Erbaugh, Mary S. 1996. "The Hakka Paradox in the People's Republic of China. Exile, Eminence, and Public Silence." In *Guest People: Hakka Identity in China and Abroad.* Edited by Nicole Constable, 196-231. Seattle: University of Washington Press.

Estanislao, Jesus P. 1992. "Finance." In *The Aquino Administration: Records and Legacy*, edited by President Corazon C. Aquino and Her Cabinet. U.P Public Lectures on the Aquino Administration and the Post -EDSA Government (1986-1992), Volume 1, 39-46. Quezon City: University of Philippines Press.

Evans, Richard. 1994. *Deng Xiaoping and the Making of Modern China*. New York: Viking.

Felix, Alfonso. Jr. 1966. "Our Approach to the Problem: How We Stand." In *The Chinese in the Philippines*, Volume 1, edited by Alfonso Felix Jr., 1-14. Manila, Philippines: Solidaridad Publishing House.

Fischer, Margaret W., Leo E. Rose, and Robert A. Huttenback. 1963. *Himalayan Battleground: Sino-Indian Rivalry in Ladakh*. London and New York: Praeger.

Franz, Uli. 1988. *Deng Xiaoping*. Translated by Tom Artin. Boston, San Diego and New York: Harcourt, Brace, Jovanovich.

Frost, Mark Ravinder, and Yu-Mei Balasingamchow. 2009. *Singapore: A Biography*. Hong Kong: Hong Kong University Press.

Gao, Tian Qiang. 1997. 圖片 香港今昔(Pictures of Hong Kong: Past and Present). 三聯書店 (Joint Publishing).

Girling, John L.S. 1993. *Interpreting Development: Capitalism, Democracy and the Middle Class in Thailand*. Vol. 21. SEAP Publications.

Grasso, June, Jay Corrin, and Michael Kort. 2009. *Modernization and Revolution in China: From the Opium Wars to the Olympics*. New York and London: M.E. Sharpe.

Griffiths, James. 2013. "India's Forgotten Chinese Internment Camp." Atlantic, August 9. http://www.theatlantic.com/china/archive/2013/08/indias-forgotten-chinese-internment-camp/278519/

Gustafsson, Bjorn A., Shi Li, and Terry Sicular (eds.). 2010. *Inequality and Public Policy in China*. New York: Cambridge University Press.

Guerrero, Milagros. C. 1966. "The Chinese in the Philippines, 1570-1770." In *The Chinese in the Philippines*, Volume 1, edited by Alfonso Felix Jr., 15-39. Manila, Philippines: Solidaridad Publishing House.

Han, Kirsten. 2012. "The Sorry State of Unions in Singapore." *Waging Non-Violence*, June 8. http://wagingnonviolence.org/feature/the-sorry-state-of-unions-in-singapore/

Hase, Patrick H. 1995. "The Alliance of Ten: Settlement and Politics in the Shataukok Area." In *Down to Earth: The Territorial Bond in South China*, edited by David Faure and Helen Siu, 123-160. Stanford, CA: Stanford University Press.

Hau, Caroline S. 2014. *The Chinese Question: Ethnicity, Nation and*

Region in and Beyond the Philippines. Singapore and Kyoto: NUS Press and Kyoto University Press.

Hewison, Kevin. 2013. "Weber, Marx, and Contemporary Thailand." *Transregional and National Studies of Southeast Asia* 1(2): 177-198. http://kevinhewison.files.wordpress.com/2011/02/hewison-2013-trans.pdf

Hoe, Yow Cheun. 2013. *Guangdong and Chinese Diaspora: The Changing Landscape of Qiaoxiang*. London and New York: Routledge.

Hunt, Luke. 2013. "End of 30-Year Hunt for Marcos Billions?" *The Diplomat*, January 8. http://thediplomat.com/2013/01/end-of-30-year-hunt-for-marcos-billions/

Jensen, Lionel M., and Timothy B. Weston (eds.). 2006. *China's Transformations: The Stories Beyond the Headlines*. Lanham, MD: Rowman and Littlefield.

Jitra, Konuntakiat. 2004. "Nam sakhun nayok thai luk chin lae thammai chueng pen... Chinnawat." [Surnames of the Thai prime ministers of Chinese descent, and why Shinawatra]. *Nation sutsapda* 611, 16-22 February.

Kiang, Clyde. 1991. *The Hakka: Search for a Homeland*. Elgin: Allegheny Press.

Lande, Carl H. 2001. "The Return of "People Power" in the Philippines." *Journal of Democracy* 12(2): 88-102.

Landow, George P. 2005. "Singapore Harbor from Its Founding to the Present: A Brief Chronology." http://web.archive.org/web/20050505081957/http://www.scholars.nus.edu.sg/post/singapore/economics/harborchron.html

Lau, C.F. 2005. "A Dialect Murders another Dialect: The Case of Hakka in Hong Kong." *International Journal of the Sociology of Language* 173: 23-35.

Lee, Khoon Choy. 2005. *Pioneers of Modern China: Understanding the Inscrutable Chinese*. Singapore: World Scientific Publishing.

Lee, Khoon Choy. 2013. *Golden Dragon and Purple Phoenix: The Chinese and Their Multi-Ethnic Descendants in Southeast Asia*. Hackensack, New Jersey: World Scientific. http://www.worldscientific.com/doi/suppl/10.1142/8357/suppl_file/8357_chap01.pdf

Lee, Kuan Yew. 1998. *The Singapore Story*. Singapore: Times Editions.

Lee, Kuan Yew. 2000. *From Third World to First: The Singapore Story: 1965-2000*. New York: Harper Collins.

Lee, Tai To, Hock Guan Lee (eds.). 2011. *Sun Yat-Sen, Nanyang and the 1911 Revolution*. Singapore: Institute of Southeast Asian Studies.

Leong, Sow-Theng. 1997. *Migration and Ethnicity in Chinese History: Hakkas, Pengmin, and Their Neighbors*. Stanford, CA: Stanford University Press.

Leung, Winnie K.L. 2012. "A Qualitative Study in the Ethnic Identification Processes of Hakka People in Hong Kong: The Role of Family Socialization among Generations of Hakka." *Discovery- SS Student E-Journal* 1: 140-153. http://ssweb.cityu.edu.hk/download/RS/E-Journal/journal7.pdf

Leyl, Sharanjit. 2012. "Singapore Uses Rap to Try to Boost Birth Rate." *BBC News*, November 29. http://www.bbc.com/news/business-20542156

Li, Shi, Hiroshi Sato, and Terry Sicular (eds.). 2013. *Rising Inequality in China: Challenges to a Harmonious Society*. New York: Cambridge University Press.

Li, Wei, and Dennis Tao Yang. 2005. "The Great Leap Forward: The Anatomy of a Central Planning Disaster." *Journal of Political Economy* 113(4): 840-877.

Lin, Rebecca, and Kai-yuan Teng. 2014. "The New Migrant Workers: Taiwan's Youth Exodus." *Commonwealth* 天下, February 20, No. 541. http://english.cw.com.tw/article.do?action=show&id=14661

Liu, Larry. 2013. "Capitalist Reform, the Dismantling of the Iron Rice Bowl and Land Expropriation in China: A Theory of Primitive Accumulation and State Power." http://www.academia.edu/5241887/Capitalist_Reform_the_Dismantling_of_the_Iron_Rice_Bowl_and_Land_Expropriation_in_China_A_Theory_of_Primitive_Accumulation_and_State_Power

Liu, Larry. 2014. "Anti-Government Protests in Thailand: A Political Sociology of Elite and Class Conflict." http://www.academia.edu/5859250/Anti-Government_Protests_In_Thailand_A_Political_Sociology_of_Elite_and_Class_Conflict

Looney, Robert. 2004. "Thaksinomics: A New Asian Paradigm?" *Journal of Social, Political and Economic Studies* 29(1): 65-82. https://relooney.fatcow.com/Rel_JSPES_04.pdf

Luo, Xianglin. 1933. *Kejia yanjiu daolun (Introduction to the Study of Hakka)*. Xinning: Xishan shucang.

Mathari, Rusdi. 2008. "Hakka, Bangsa dari Kerajaan Surga dan Bumi." *Rusdi Goblog*, February 5. http://rusdimathari.wordpress.com/2008/02/05/hakka-bangsa-dari-kerajaan-surga-dan-bumi/

Mazumdar, Jaideep. 2010. "The 1962 Jailing of Chinese Indians." *Open*

Magazine, November 20.
http://www.openthemagazine.com/article/nation/the-1962-jailing-of-chinese-indians

Merrill, Tim. 1992. *Guyana and Belize: Country Studies*. Washington D.C.: Federal Research Division, Library of Congress.

Michael, Franz. 1966. *The Taiping Rebellion: History and Documents*. Seattle: University of Washington Press.

Minahan, James. 2014. *Ethnic Groups of North, East and Central Asia: An Encyclopedia*. Santa Barbara, CA: ABC-CLIO.

Naughton, Barry. 1995. *Growing out of the Plan: Chinese Economic Reforms: 1978-1993*. New York: Cambridge University Press.

Ng, Y.L. 1983. *New Peace County: A Chinese Gazetteer of the Hong Kong Region*. Hong Kong: Hong Kong University Press.

Omar, Marsita, and Fook Weng Chan. 2009. "British Withdrawal from Singapore." *Singapore Infopedia*. http://eresources.nlb.gov.sg/infopedia/articles/SIP_1001_2009-02-10.html

Oxfeld, Ellen. 1993. *Blood, Sweat and Mahjong: Family and Enterprise in an Overseas Chinese Community*. Ithaca, NY: Cornell University Press.

Pathmanand, Ukrist. 1998. "The Thaksin Shinawatra Group: A Study of the Relationship between Money and Politics in Thailand." *Copenhagen Journal of Asian Studies* 13(98): 60-81.

Pathmanand, Ukrist. 2001. "Globalization and Democratic Development in Thailand: The New Path of the Military, the Private Sector, and Civil Society." *Contemporary Southeast Asia* 23(1): 24-42.

Phongpaichit, Pasuk, and Chris Baker. 2009. *Thaksin: Second edition*. Chiang Mai: Silkworm Books.

Plaior, Chananon. 1987. *Pho kha kap phatthanakan rabop thun niyom nai phak nuea pho. so. 2464-2523. [Traders and development of capitalism in the north, 1921-80]*. Bangkok: CUSRI.

Prani, Sirithorn Na Phattalung. 1980. *Phu bukboek haeng chiangmai. [Pioneers of Chiangmai]*. Bangkok: Krirk University.

Rajaretnam, M. 1986. "Questions and Answers." In *The Aquino Alternative*, edited by M. Rajaretnam, 125-156. Singapore: Institute of Southeast Asian Studies.

Reid, Robert H., and Eileen Guerrero. 1995. *Corazon Aquino and the Brushfire Revolution*. Baton Rouge and London: Louisiana State University Press.

Reilly, Thomas H. 2004. *The Taiping Heavenly Kingdom: Rebellion and the Blasphemy of Empire*. Seattle and London: University of Washington Press.

Richter, Linda K. 1991. "Exploring Theories of Female Leadership in

South and Southeast Asia." *Pacific Affairs* 63(4): 524-540.
Roberts, J.A.G. 2003. *The Complete History of China*. Glucestershire, UK: Sutton Publishing.
Schrock, Joann L., Irene Crowe, Marilou Fromme, Dennis E. Gosier, Virginia S. McKenzie, Raymond W. Myers, and Patricia Stegeman. 1970. *Minority Groups in Thailand: Ethnographic Study Series*. Washington D.C.: US Government Printing Office.
Seagrave, Sterling. 1988. *The Marcos Dynasty*. New York: Harper and Row.
Shawki, Ahmed. 1997. "China: From Mao to Deng." *International Socialist Review,* Issue 1.
http://www.isreview.org/issues/01/mao_to_deng_1.shtml
Shinawatra, Thaksin. 1999. *Thaksin Chinnawat: Ta du dao thao tit din. [Thaksin Shinawatra: Eyes on the stars, feet on the ground]*. Edited by Walaya. Bangkok: Matichon.
Shiraishi, Takashi. 2014. "Changing Fortunes: Comparing State Building and Economic Development in Indonesia, the Philippines, Thailand, and Malaysia." In *State Building and Development*, edited by Keijiro Otsuka and Takashi Shiraishi, 73-94. New York: Routledge.
Siamwalla, Ammar. 1980. "An Economic Theory of Patron-Client Relationships: With some Examples from Thailand." Paper for Thai-European Seminar on Social Change in Contemporary Thailand, Amsterdam, May.
Sison, Jose Ma. 1986. "Current Questions Concerning the Communist Party of the Philippines." In *The Aquino Alternative*, edited by M. Rajaretnam, 54-66. Singapore: Institute of Southeast Asian Studies.
Situ, Andrew. 2014. "Singapore's Prime Minister Sues Blogger for a Pound of Flesh." *The Real Singapore*, July 2.
http://therealsingapore.com/content/singapore%E2%80%99s-prime-minister-sues-blogger-pound-flesh
Skinner, G. William. 1958. *Leadership and Power in The Chinese Community of Thailand*. Ithaca, NY: Cornell University Press.
Sorakon, Adulyanon. 1993. *Thaksin Chinnawat asawin khloen luk thi sam [Thaksin Shinawatra, knight of the third wave]*. Bangkok: Matichon.
Suarez, Thomas. 1999. *Early Mapping of Southeast Asia*. Singapore: Periplus Editions.
Sue-A-Quan, Trev. 2000. "The Experiences of Early Hakka Immigrants in Guyana: An Account of four Families." Paper presented at the Hakka Conference, Toronto.
http://guyaneseonline.files.wordpress.com/2013/11/chinese-

in-guyana-four-hakka-families.pdf

Sun, Yan. 2004. *Corruption and Market in Contemporary China*. Ithaca, NY: Cornell University Press.

Suryadinata, Leo. 2013. "Southeast Asian Policies toward the Ethnic Chinese." In *Routledge Handbook of the Chinese Diaspora*, edited by Tan Chee-Beng. London and New York: Routledge.

Tan Bi'an. 1963. "Sun Zhongshan jiashi yuanliu ji qi shangdai jingji zhuangjuang xinzheng." (New Evidence on Sun Yat-sen's ancestry and his ancestors' economic situation.") *Xueshu Yanjiu (Academic Research)* 3: 32-38.

Teiwes, Frederick C., and Warren Sun. 1999. *China's Road to Disaster: Mao, Central Politicians, and Provincial Leaders in the Unfolding of the Great Leap Forward, 1955-1959*. No. 24. Armonk, NY: ME Sharpe.

Teng, S.Y. 1971. *The Taiping Rebellion and the Western Powers: A Comprehensive Survey*. London: Oxford University Press.

Terwiel, B.J. 2011. *Thailand's Political History: From the 13th Century to Recent Times*. Bangkok: River Books.

Thompson, Mark R. 2014. "The Politics Philippine President Make." *Critical Asian Studies* 46(3): 433-460.

Tsa, Shih-Shan Henry. 2005. *Lee Teng-hui and Taiwan's Quest for Identity*. New York: Palgrave Macmillan.

Tumcharoen, Surasak. 2009. "A Very Distinguished Province." *Translate Thai*, December 3. http://thaitranslated.blogspot.com/2009/12/very-distinguished-province.html

Turnbull, C. M. 2009. *A History of Modern Singapore: 1819-2005*. Singapore: National University of Singapore Press.

Tyler, Patrick E. 1996. "Taiwan's Leader Wins Its Election and a Mandate." *New York Times*, March 24. http://www.nytimes.com/1996/03/24/world/taiwan-s-leader-wins-its-election-and-a-mandate.html

UN. 2004. "Promotion and Protection of Human Rights: Human Rights Defenders. Addendum: Mission to Thailand." United Nations Commission on Human Rights. March.

Van den Broek, Matthijs. 2012. "Asia's Power Women Offer False Hope." *Business Trends Asia Blog*, August 27. http://businesstrendsasia.blogspot.com/2012_08_01_archive.html

Vogel, Ezra F. 2011. *Deng Xiaoping and the Transformation of China*. Cambridge, MA and London: Harvard University Press.

Wang, Qingcheng. 1992. "Kejia yu Taiping Tianguo qiyi." (The Hakkas and the Taiping Uprising). In *Zhongguo Kejia minxi yanjiu (Research on the Hakkas of China.)*, edited by Qiu Quanzheng,

264-275. Beijing: Zhongguo Gongren Chubanshe.
Wang, Qingcheng. 1994. "Kejia yu Taiping Tianguo qiyi." (The Hakkas and the Taiping Uprising). In *Guoji kejiaxue yantaohui lunwenji (The Proceedings of the International Conference on Hakkaology)*, edited by Xie Jian and Zheng Chiyan, 819-826. Xianggang: Xianggang Zhongwen Daxue.
Weathers, Frank. 2012. "Singapore and the Strange Tale of Population Control Policies Updates." *Patheos*, August 9. http://www.patheos.com/blogs/yimcatholic/2012/08/singapor e-and-the-strange-tale-of-population-control-policies.html
Wederman, Andrew. 2004. "The Intensification of Corruption in China." *China Quarterly* 180: 895-921.
Wong, Hongyi. 2009. "Lim Chin Siong." *Singapore Infopedia*. http://eresources.nlb.gov.sg/infopedia/articles/SIP_1462_200 9-02-18.html
Xie, Tingyu. 1929. "Origin and Migrations of the Hakkas." *Chinese Social and Political Science Review* 13: 202-227. http://pages.ucsd.edu/~dkjordan/chin/HsiehHakkaHistory.ht ml
Xie, Lizhong (ed.). 2014. *De-Politicization of Ethnic Questions in China*. Singapore: World Scientific.
Yip, Bennis So Wai. 2006. "Privatisation." In *Critical Issues in Contemporary China*, edited by Czeslaw Tubilewicz, 49-78. Oxon, UK: Routledge.
Zeng, Fanxing. 2004. "Hakka and Huaren Destiny, Challenge and Response." *World Huaren Federation*. http://www.huaren.org/members-contribution/hakka--huaren
Zhang, Xinghan. 1994. "Tan'Tan Shezu yu Hanzu Kejia minxi de wenhua hudong guanxi' (On the Reciprocal Relationship Between the She Nationality and the Hakka Descent Group of the Han Nationality). In *Shezu lishi yu wenhua (History and Culture of the She Nationality)*, edited by Shi Lianzhu and Lei Wenxian, 128-142. Beijing: Zhongyang Minzu Daxue Chubanshe.

Photo Credit: "Meeting between Deng Xiaoping, Lee Kuan Yew Depicted in China TV Serial." August 28, 2014. If Only Singaporeans Stopped to Think Blog. http://ifonlysingaporeans.blogspot.com/2014/08/meeting-between-deng-xiaoping-lee-kuan.html

Index

About the Author:

L.(Liam Ching) Larry Liu is an undergraduate in the University of Pennsylvania, studying sociology and economic policy, and currently resides in Philadelphia. His research interests besides Hakka history and politics include the political economy of Europe, comparative labor market institutions, economic history of developed countries, political sociology and class relations in East and Southeast Asia, technological effects on employment, inequality and social stratification, among others.

A few examples of his work include
"Anti-Government Protests in Thailand: A Political
    Sociology of Elite and Class Conflict." *Penn Asian
    Review* 4 (2014): 18-23.
*The Austerity Trap: Economic and Social Consequences of
    Fiscal Consolidation in Europe.* Charleston, SC:
    CreateSpace (2015).
"Salesworkers in the Twenty-First Century: The Effects of
    Technological Change on Retail and Financial
    Service Employment." Independent Study,
    University of Pennsylvania, Department of Sociology.
    April 2014.
"Codetermination: Trade Union Power in Germany and the
    US." Sociology of Law Course, University of
    Pennsylvania, Department of Sociology. February
    2014.

He can be reached by e-mail for critiques and comments:
    liam.ching.liu@gmail.com

21558573R00075

Made in the USA
Middletown, DE
12 December 2018